MUHAMMAD ALI

Other Books by Ralph Oates

A Question of Boxing (2021)

A Round of Boxing: A Trip Through Time (2019)

Bruno and Lewis: The Boxing Years (2017)

The Noble Art of Heavyweight Boxing (2015)

The World Champions Boxing Quiz Book (2013)

The Ultimate Boxing Quiz Book (2009)

The Muhammad Ali Boxing Quiz Book (2007)

The Heavyweight Boxing Quiz Book (2000)

Boxing Shadows: 1500 Boxing Quiz Questions (1997)

Boxing Clever (1994)

Know Your Boxing (1991)

World Heavyweight Boxing Champions Elite (1987)

MUHAMMAD ALI
The Man Who Changed Boxing

Ralph Oates

WHITE OWL
AN IMPRINT OF PEN & SWORD BOOKS LTD.
YORKSHIRE - PHILADELPHIA

First published in Great Britain in 2024 by
PEN AND SWORD WHITE OWL
An imprint of
Pen & Sword Books Ltd
Yorkshire – Philadelphia

Copyright © Ralph Oates, 2024

ISBN 978 1 39904 726 5

The right of Ralph Oates to be identified as Author of this work has been asserted by him in accordance with the Copyright, Designs and Patents Act 1988.

A CIP catalogue record for this book is available from the British Library.

All rights reserved. No part of this book may be reproduced or transmitted in any form or by any means, electronic or mechanical including photocopying, recording or by any information storage and retrieval system, without permission from the Publisher in writing.

Typeset in Times New Roman 11.5/14 by
SJmagic DESIGN SERVICES, India.
Printed and bound in the UK by CPI Group (UK) Ltd, Croydon, CR0 4YY.

Pen & Sword Books Limited incorporates the imprints of Atlas, Archaeology, Aviation, Discovery, Family History, Fiction, History, Maritime, Military, Military Classics, Politics, Select, Transport, True Crime, Air World, Frontline Publishing, Leo Cooper, Remember When, Seaforth Publishing, The Praetorian Press, Wharncliffe Local History, Wharncliffe Transport, Wharncliffe True Crime, White Owl and After the Battle.

For a complete list of Pen & Sword titles please contact

PEN & SWORD BOOKS LIMITED
George House, Units 12 & 13, Beevor Street, Off Pontefract Road,
Barnsley, South Yorkshire, S71 1HN, England
E-mail: enquiries@pen-and-sword.co.uk
Website: www.pen-and-sword.co.uk

or

PEN AND SWORD BOOKS
1950 Lawrence Rd, Havertown, PA 19083, USA
E-mail: uspen-and-sword@casematepublishers.com
Website: www.penandswordbooks.com

Dedicated to the memory of Ruby Oates
who was a very special lady

Contents

Foreword ix

About the Author x

Acknowledgements xi

Professional Boxing Organisations xii

Introduction xiii

Chapter 1   The Beginning 1

Chapter 2   Paid Ranks 5

Chapter 3   Fights in Los Angeles 11

Chapter 4   Clay Beats Cooper 20

Chapter 5   Shocks the World 30

Chapter 6   Another World Heavyweight Title Bout in the USA 34

Chapter 7   A New Name 38

Chapter 8   Stripped of the WBA Title 42

Chapter 9   Ali Meets Cooper for a Second Time 48

Chapter 10 London Challenges Ali 54

Chapter 11 Ali Defends Against Mildenberger 60

Chapter 12 Undisputed World Champion 64

Muhammad Ali: The Man Who Changed Boxing

Chapter 13   Frazier and Ellis become Champions 69

Chapter 14   Ali Meets with Defeat 76

Chapter 15   Ali Captures the NABF Title 81

Chapter 16   Defeated for a Second Time 87

Chapter 17   Ali Regains World Heavyweight Title 93

Chapter 18   Foreman Returns to the Ring 100

Chapter 19   Bugner Challenges Ali for the World Heavyweight Title 105

Chapter 20   Ali and Frazier Meet for a Third Time 110

Chapter 21   Ali Defeats another Briton 115

Chapter 22   Ali Shocked by Spinks 121

Chapter 23   Ali Back on Top of the World 127

Chapter 24   The Last Contest 132

Chapter 25   Ali Returns to the Olympic Games 136

Chapter 26   The World Bids Farewell to Ali 140

Bibliography 143

Index 144

Foreword

My first contact with Ralph Oates came about in 2008, when he wrote an article about my boxing career in *The British Boxing Board of Control Yearbook*. When Ralph recently contacted me and asked if I would like to write a foreword for his latest book, *Muhammad Ali: The Man Who Changed Boxing*, I was delighted to do so.

Ali was, of course, a true great; there can be no argument about that. And Ali did, of course, change boxing in many ways and in so doing really enhanced the sport. This book, which is presented in an easy to read way about the former three-time world heavyweight king, is an enjoyable, fact-filled publication. I am sure fight fans will enjoy this latest offering from Ralph.

Colin McMillan, BEM
Former WBO World, British (two-time) and
Commonwealth featherweight champion

A note on Colin's outstanding fight career

On 16 May 1992, Colin challenged Italy's Maurizio Stecca for the WBO featherweight crown. The Briton looked to be in for a tough fight against a very talented title holder who was also a former gold medallist, having found success at the 1984 Lost Angeles Olympic Games in the bantamweight division. However, Colin gave an outstanding performance to take the title and gave British boxing a boost on the night.

About the Author

Ralph, a former amateur boxer, has previously written twelve books on boxing. Over the past twenty-six years, he has also written articles for *The British Boxing Board of Control Year Book* – the leading book of its kind. He has contributed to the magazines *My Planet Liverpool* and *Beyond*, and has had his own boxing column in the *Essex Courier*, the monthly paper *Take One*, and monthly magazine *Bounce*. At present, Ralph writes a boxing column for the *Cardiff Times*. He is also a former boxing consultant for Guinness World Records, and has compiled questions for the national TV quiz show *Who Dares Wins*.

Ralph is donating his royalties from the sale of this book to The Ringside Charitable Trust. The aim of the charity is to provide a residential home for ex-boxers to be cared for when they meet various difficulties after they retire from the sport.

Acknowledgements

In putting this book together, I would like to thank for his assistance my brother, Howard Oates, who helped to check the facts that appear in the publication. This is by no means an easy task. Also thanks to my sister-in-law, Denise Oates, for her technical advice. Further thanks must also go to the excellent photographers who contributed the images for the book: Derek Rowe and Philip Sharkey – two men who are the best in their field and constantly producing top quality images.

My thanks also to Colin McMillan for taking the time to write the foreword. Colin is a well-respected fighter who, during his time in boxing, won the WBO, British (twice) and Commonwealth featherweight titles.

Last and by no means least, I would also like to thank all at Pen and Sword for their fantastic help and guidance in producing this book.

Professional Boxing Organisations

BBB of C	British Boxing Board of Control
IBA	International Boxing Association
IBF	International Boxing Federation
IWBF	International Women's Boxing Federation
NABF	North American Boxing Federation
NBA	National Boxing Association
NYSAC	New York State Athletic Commission
WBA	World Boxing Association
WBC	World Boxing Council
WBF	World Boxing Federation
WBU	World Boxing Union
WIBA	Women's International Boxing Association
WIBF	Women's International Boxing Federation

Introduction

When Muhammad Ali (then named Cassius Clay) arrived on the boxing scene no one could have foreseen the impact this young fighter would make in the sport in the years to follow. I remember reading about Ali in the newspapers prior to his first meeting with Sonny Liston. Being an amateur boxer myself at the time, his persona really interested me, as it did so many others. It was apparent that he was an excellent boxer and had a good career ahead of him. How good a career it was going to be was a matter of opinion, depending on whom you spoke to. Boxing is a precarious profession, where one punch can change the direction of a fighter's course in an instant.

When a highly decorated amateur turns to the professional ranks, all eyes are upon him watching his progress keenly, especially if he is a heavyweight. The heavyweights are always good business; when a good one comes along, he will be of great interest and quickly signed up by a leading manager. The heavyweight will pull in the punters, ensuring a healthy box-office return for the promoter. There is a degree of pressure put on the fighter by public expectations. Ali, an Olympic gold medal winner, looked like championship material from the start and if he did feel any pressure during his foray into professional boxing, it certainly didn't show. He always appeared in control and untroubled, able to handle any situation that might come his way inside the ring.

Admittedly, it was not all plain sailing for Ali during his fighting career or indeed his personal life outside of the roped arena. He would often walk hand in hand with controversy; his views on a number of issues inside and outside of the sport upset many people who did not agree with him. Make no mistake, Ali was his own man and called it how he saw it, and if you didn't like what he said, well that was too bad. He had his point of view and he was sticking to it, no matter what. Despite this, even his sternest critics would have to admit that he brought something new to boxing, something fresh that had not been seen before. He lit up the game and gave it a fresh look. Ali was so confident making predictions about the round in which his opponent would be defeated that often such predictions came true. He would make derogatory comments about his opponents before a fight. He was the master of playing mind games and some would say, psychologically, he won many fights before he even stepped into the ring to do battle.

Ali was, in the beginning of his professional career, both loved and hated by fans in equal measure. Was he a villain or a hero? Was he joking or was he serious when making outrageous statements? At the time, many were not sure. It is no secret that a number of people wanted to see this arrogant and boastful young man get beaten in his early days, wanted to see him put firmly in his place by some of the opposition he faced in the ring. I well remember speaking to a fight follower a number of years ago when Ali was starting out and he expressed in no uncertain terms that Ali was all talk and an attention seeker who would never become a world champion. He went on to add that it was only a matter of time before he 'is found out, exposed as a fraud and is well beaten'. He would then disappear from the sport, never to be seen or heard of again. Well, he certainly got that one wrong, big time!

Whatever your view on Ali you couldn't ignore him, that's for sure. There is a saying that if you talk the talk, you have to walk the walk. Well, Ali could certainly walk the walk. Ali showed this throughout his career, and he had the courage in battle to complement his fine boxing skills. Inside the ring, there is no hiding place and there comes a moment when every fighter is put to the supreme test. They may well have been hyped up by the publicity and their management team, but that counts for very little when they meet an opponent on the same level who has the same ambition. Many highly rated prospects in the past have been found wanting when put to the test, and could not live up to the hype that surrounded them.

Make no mistake, Ali was often tested and showed that he had the heart and desire to overcome the biggest obstacles put in front of him. He would go into the trenches and battle hard when it was necessary, fighting fire with fire. He took on every available contender when holding the world title; they were all given their chance at the championship. Ali had this remarkable ability of being able to defy the odds, often going into the lion's den to fight his opponent on their own turf. In so

Introduction

doing, he fought in a number of different countries during his career. In fact, he boxed and defended his title abroad more often than any previous American world heavyweight titleholder did. His incredible speed of punch and ability to avoid the gloves coming in his direction was truly amazing. He showed that he was able to take a punch when one penetrated his defence. His recuperative power was impressive. He clearly did not have a glass jaw, which was just as well since he locked horns with some of the most explosive punchers in the ring – punchers who had a reputation of putting their opponents' lights out should they land on target. Every boxer, no matter how fast or agile they may be, will have to take a solid punch when competing at one time or another. That is part of the sport and it comes with the territory. It is good to hit without being hit, but that is impossible. Boxers punch and boxers get punched, that's the way it works. To use the old expression: you can't take a shower without getting wet, and Ali did get wet a few times during his bouts.

Over the years, Ali earned the respect of his fellow boxers and, of course, the public at large, whom he eventually won over with his performances. He became very popular in the UK, where he had many fans, be it on talk shows or when performing in the ring. Even when faced with and defeating British challengers, he still gained the admiration and respect of the Brits. There is no doubt that Ali brought a great deal of interest and freshness to heavyweight boxing at a time when it really needed it. He was remarkable in so many ways; he was so sure that he was meant to become the world heavyweight champion – not just *a* world champion but *a great* world champion, the best there had ever been in the history of the sport.

It soon become apparent that Ali was not only a boxer, he was also an entertainer who could be charming and funny, and perhaps most importantly, a showman who could sell a fight to the public. He held the attention of those who previously had no interest in boxing. He more than likely brought new fans to the sport with his antics. He was far from dull; he had a zest for life that shone like a bright light through the darkness. Whether fighting in the ring or appearing in TV interviews, he stole the show. The media could not get enough of this man; his every comment was noted and recorded in the newspapers. He truly transcended the sport in a big way. Ali featured on many magazine front covers over the years, such was the interest the public had in him.

Muhammad Ali: The Man Who Changed Boxing

The fight game had not seen anything like him before and it is possible that his like will never again be seen representing the sport.

Every now and then in boxing, as indeed in many other sports, someone special comes along and Ali was indeed special – very special. He proved to be a tonic, a lifesaver for a sport that was becoming far too predictable and old hat. It was a real occasion whenever Ali fought: he was magnetic, a compulsive watch, and you never knew what was coming or what he was going to say next. He had a range of opinions on many subjects apart from boxing, which duly revealed his intelligence. He was a boxer who did not conform to the widely held perception of how a fighter should act. Quite simply, he did not fit the stereotype that the public had previously held about boxers. Ali was a one-off, an original who could not be replicated. Some fighters attempted to mimic his style in the ring but to no avail.

Joe Louis was a legend, a well-respected fighter who held the record in boxing for making the most successive defences of the world heavyweight title during his time as champion – twenty-five in all. That was no mean feat. I firmly believe that had Ali not been robbed of his peak years during the dispute over his conscription into the US Army, he would have surpassed Louis's record. The man from Louisville might even have left the sport with an undefeated slate had he maintained his momentum and kept fighting. However, Ali made difficult choices during his life and took the hard road rather than the easy road. He had to be respected for staying true to his beliefs no matter what the consequences were likely to be … and there were consequences. The decisions made by Ali did of course cost him dearly in a number of ways.

During his time, Ali participated in twenty-five world title bouts as both challenger and champion, winning twenty-two and losing three. The heavyweight division over the years has produced a number of other outstanding fighters who also provided exciting moments in the ring. Ali would often say that he was the greatest of them all. Now that may or may not be true, depending on your point of view. However, it was a bold statement to make, which, as one would expect, upset a number of fans. Indeed, amongst followers of the fight game, this created many a heated debate about Ali's abilities and how he would have fared against the likes of Jack Johnson, Joe Louis, Rocky Marciano, Ezzard Charles, Jersey Joe Walcott, Jack Dempsey and Gene Tunney. Debates, arguments, heated discussions, call them what you will, but whatever

Introduction

opinion was ever reached on the subject was a pointless exercise for the only way to know for sure was for Ali to have faced these men in the ring, and that, for obvious reasons, didn't happen.

The situation has now gone full circle. Many fans now wonder how the heavyweights who came in later years would have fared against Ali. Fighters like world champions Mike Tyson, Evander Holyfield and Lennox Lewis, who now rank with the greats in the division. More recent fighters like Tyson Fury, Anthony Joshua, Deontay Wilder and Oleksandr Usyk can also been added to the mix.

Ali, of course, went on far too long and had that one fight too many, like so many fighters had before him. It would have been fantastic to have seen him bow out on a winning note, a winner from start to finish. That would have been an ideal finale to his boxing career. However, I think everyone would agree that the end of his career, which saw him lose twice in a row, did not define or ruin his legacy in any way whatsoever. Ali was obviously past his best in his later ring outings. Sadly, he became a mere ghost of the fighter he once was, attempting to capture the past, hoping to find that one golden moment when he could turn the clock back and produce one more outstanding performance. His ageing body was not able to perform the way it once had in his youth. The sands of time had run out – even the best of fighters cannot outbox time.

At his best, Ali was a sight to behold – a truly unbeatable boxing master who had the ring intelligence to overcome the very best put in front of him. Such was his supreme skill, he was able to outpunch and outthink his opponents. In future years, there will be other heavyweight fighters considered great, who have their unique style, and who can capture the imagination of a new generation of fight fans. But none of those who follow Ali will ever have the kind of magic he possessed during his time in the ring. It is a tribute to him that even today, his name is well respected, and the passing of time has not dimmed the enormous contribution he made to the sport. He showed that boxing is indeed a form of art; a number of his performances were poetry in motion.

To get back to the word 'great', in recent years the term in boxing has been somewhat abused by being used to acknowledge good performances but hardly those that can be called great. Indeed, how do you measure boxing greatness; what barometer do you use to do so? Do you gauge a fighter on the class of opposition he met and defeated?

Muhammad Ali: The Man Who Changed Boxing

The number of times he successfully defended his title? The number of times he overcame the odds to win in what appeared to be a mission impossible? Whatever scale is used, I believe Ali by his very record ticks every required box. His achievements are truly great within an outstanding fighting career. His legacy will forever be a very important part of boxing history.

Muhammad Ali: The Man Who Changed Boxing does not pretend to be Ali's life story, but it aims to present the most fascinating facts around him, as well as around those who have been associated with him through the years in one capacity or another. It is presented in an easy-to-read format, whereby the reader can dip into any page to find a fact of interest. I hope you enjoy the book and gain rounds of pleasure through reading it.

Ralph Oates

Chapter 1

The Beginning

The birth of Cassius Clay

Cassius Marcellus Clay was born on 17 January 1942 at the General Hospital in Louisville, Kentucky, USA. The weight of the newborn baby was a reported 6 pounds and 7 ounces. His proud parents were Odessa Grady Clay and Cassius Clay Snr.

Young Clay's life was shaped by the fact that he grew up knowing the stress of living in times of racial segregation. The situation whilst far from being pleasant made him determined to succeed in life and overcome the many difficulties that he would have to face. On 18 July 1944, the Clay household welcomed a new addition to the family when Rudolph Valentino Clay was born. Like his older brother Cassius, Rudolph would take up the sport of boxing, eventually changing his name to Rahman (Rahaman) Ali.

Joe Louis

At the time of Cassius Clay's birth, the reigning world heavyweight champion was Joe Louis. Louis was nicknamed the Brown Bomber and at the time was recognised as one of the greats in the history of the sport.

Clay's introduction to boxing

Serving police officer Joe E. Martin is the man credited with introducing Cassius Clay to the sport of boxing. The two men met when Clay had his bike stolen and wanted to get even with the culprits, whereupon Martin persuaded the young man in front of him to join a boxing club. In the course of time, Clay won a number of amateur titles, leading him eventually to the Olympic Games.

Muhammad Ali: The Man Who Changed Boxing

First amateur contest

The first fight for any boxer is a moment he will remember for the rest of his life; be it as the winner or loser, the memory will always remain with him. The first time stepping between the ropes and into the ring is magical. Cassius Clay must have felt this emotion when he reportedly had his first amateur contest against opponent Ronnie O'Keefe, whom he outpointed over the duration of three rounds on 12 November 1954 at the WAVE-TV Studio in Louisville, Kentucky.

First amateur defeat

Cassius Clay reportedly suffered his first amateur defeat in his fifth bout on 28 July 1955, when opponent John Hampton outpointed him over three rounds at the Audubon Country Club in Louisville, Kentucky. This was a reversal of fortunes, for in their previous meeting on 22 July 1955 at the WAVE-TV Studio in Louisville, Clay had outpointed Hampton over three rounds.

Olympic gold medal, 1960

Cassius Clay gained international prominence when he won the gold medal in the light-heavyweight division at the 1960 Olympic Games in Rome, Italy. He outpointed his southpaw opponent Zbigniew Pietrzykowski of Poland over of three rounds. Pietrzykowski was an accomplished boxer who had previously competed in the 1956 Games, which had taken place in Melbourne, Australia. On that occasion, he gained a bronze medal in the light-middleweight poundage.

Impressive win by Clay

On his way towards the light-heavyweight gold medal in the 1960 Olympic Games, Cassius Clay defeated opponent Gennadiy Shatkov of the Soviet Union in the quarter-finals. He secured the win with a points victory over three rounds. This was an impressive win for the American. In the 1956 Games, in Melbourne, Shatkov had won the gold medal at middleweight.

On the medal podium

On the 1960 medal podium with gold medal winner Cassius Clay was Zbigniew Pietrzykowski from Poland, who won the silver medal. The two bronze medallists were Giulio Saraudi (Italy) and Anthony Madigan (Australia).

Clay, the fourth

On defeating Zbigniew Pietrzykowski at the 1960 Olympic Games, Cassius Clay became only the fourth boxer from the USA to win a gold medal in the light-heavyweight division. The first was Eddie Eagan, who accomplished the honour at the 1920 Games in Antwerp, Belgium. The second was Norvel Lee, who captured gold in 1952 at the Helsinki Games. Third was Jim Boyd, who boxed his way to gold at the 1956 event, which took place at Melbourne, Australia.

Three boxers from the USA

Cassius Clay was one of three boxers from the USA to win a gold medal at the 1960 Olympic Games, which were held in Rome, Italy. The other two were Wilbert McClure, at light-middleweight, and Eddie Crook Jr, middleweight. Clay was the only one of the three to eventually go on to win a world championship in the professional ranks. Crook Jr stayed amateur whilst McClure turned professional.

McClure was not short of talent but did not succeed at top level. He eventually retired from the sport after being stopped in round ten in a contest that took place against Billy Douglas on 31 January 1970. The venue for the McClure–Douglas bout was the Fairgrounds Coliseum, Detroit, Michigan. McClure had comprised a resume of thirty-three fights during his career, winning twenty-four and losing eight, with one drawn.

1964 Olympic Games

After losing to Cassius Clay, Zbigniew Pietrzykowski continued his boxing journey. He took part in his third Olympic Games in 1964, hoping to win that elusive gold medal, in Tokyo, Japan. His ambition and drive to capture the top prize had to be admired. On this occasion, Pietrzykowski participated once again in the light-heavyweight division. It is often said that third time's a charm, but not in this case. Pietrzykowski, much to his disappointment, failed to obtain the top spot on the podium. He came up against Aleksei Kiselyov of the Soviet Union, who outpointed him over three rounds in the semi-final. The defeat saw Pietrzykowski having to settle for a bronze medal to add to his Olympic awards collection. All things considered, Pietrzykowski did very well during his amateur career, despite his not being able to win gold.

Chapter 2

Paid Ranks

Professional debut

After his success at the 1960 Olympic Games, Cassius Clay turned to the professional ranks and made his much-anticipated debut on 29 October 1960. Turning professional was the obvious move since Clay had nothing more to prove in the amateurs. The ex-gold medallist was managed by a group of Louisville businessmen headed by Bill Faversham. They liked what they saw in young Clay and felt he had a good future ahead of him – one that was full of promise. Clay in his first outing was matched against opponent Tunney Hunsaker, who came into the ring with a resume of twenty-seven fights, winning seventeen and losing nine, with one drawn. Hunsaker had lost his last six bouts in a row, which suggested he was not likely to throw a spanner in the works and spoil Clay's debut. Hunsaker was a sensible choice of opponent for Clay since he was not too tough and not too easy an adversity to meet – the ideal opponent, in fact, for a fighter who was taking part in his first bout. The fight took place at the Freedom Hall, Louisville, Kentucky. The contest saw Clay gain a six-round points victory over Hunsaker. The fight did not produce any real fireworks of any description, which disappointed some fans who expected a more sensational start to his career. An explosive win inside the distance would have been much more to their liking. However, a win's a win, and that is what counts at the end of the day.

First promoter

The promoter of the Cassius Clay–Tunney Hunsaker contest was Bill King. Thus, King went on record as being the first man to promote a professional fight that involved Clay.

Paul Matchuny

Paul Matchuny was the third man in the ring when Cassius Clay and Tunney Hunsaker fought. This may not have seemed anything to get too excited about at the time, but later events showed that it was indeed a special moment, since the debutant went on to achieve great things in the ring. Matchuny hence had the distinction of becoming the first man to referee a professional contest in which Clay had taken part.

Two judges

Sidney Baer and Walter Beck sat ringside at the Cassius Clay and Tunney Hunsaker contest. In so doing, they became the first judges to officiate at a professional contest that involved Clay. It is doubtful whether Baer and Beck realised at the time that they were judging a future great world heavyweight champion in action.

Irony

It is somewhat ironic when you consider that the man who introduced Cassius Clay to boxing was Joe E. Martin, a serving police office. Then, later, Clay's first professional opponent, Tunney Hunsaker, was also a serving police officer.

First professional win inside the distance

Cassius Clay won his first professional contest inside the scheduled distance on 27 December 1960 in his second outing. The bout, scheduled for eight rounds, took place at the Auditorium, Miami Beach, Florida, against opponent Herb Siler, who took to the ring with a record of six fights, with five wins and one defeat. That was not a bad resume. In his fight before meeting Clay, Siler had beaten Tommy Stru on 26 October 1960 at the Auditorium, Miami Beach, outpointing him over six rounds. His last defeat had taken place on 7 June 1960, when Tony Alongi stopped him in the fourth round of six. Once again, the venue for that bout was the Auditorium, Miami Beach. Since that setback, Siler had won three fights in succession, so he was obviously back in the game and ready to rock 'n' roll. It really looked as if he might very well give Clay a run for his money. That was wishful thinking, to say the least. Siler was on the receiving end for most of the contest. The undefeated fighter was on another level, a much higher level than that of the opposition he was confronting in the ring that night. Clay gave a masterful performance, always being that one step in front of his opponent. He closed the show in round four of a scheduled eight when the referee stepped in to stop the bout in his favour.

Happy birthday

On 17 January 1961, Cassius Clay climbed into the ring at the Auditorium, Miami Beach, to face opponent Tony Esperti, who came with a slate of sixteen fights consisting of nine wins and five defeats, with two drawn. Esperti had lost his last three bouts in a row. Before taking on Clay, he had last ventured into the ring on 21 March 1955. On that occasion, he lost a four-round points decision to Al Anderson at the Eastern Parkway Arena, Brooklyn, New York. When considering his long absence from the ring, it really wasn't likely that Esperti would change the course of Clay's career by scoring an unexpected win. When the bell sounded to start the fight it soon became clear that Esperti was not in his opponent's league; he had no answer to the educated fists of Clay and was stopped in the third stanza. The contest was scheduled for the duration of eight rounds. Clay had now increased his undefeated record to three. On this day, Clay also celebrated his nineteenth birthday. So one assumes, following his fast victory over Esperti, that he was able to arrive home in good time to blow out the candles on his cake. This was the first and only time that Clay fought in the professional ranks on the day he celebrated his birth.

First one-round win

It was back to sunny Florida on 7 February 1961, when, at the Convention Center, Miami Beach, Cassius Clay in his fourth professional outing had an early night. Any fighter would welcome an early night when fighting, especially if he's the on the winning side. Clay scored his first win in the opening round in a contest scheduled for eight without raising a sweat or his pulse rate. The opponent who succumbed in the opening stanza was Jimmy Robinson, who entered the ring with a record of fourteen fights, winning six and losing six, with two drawn.

Robinson, before lacing up the gloves to step in with Clay, had fought on 6 December 1960. That particular visit to the ring proved to be a successful one when he outpointed Harry Bellefonte over six rounds. The venue for the Robinson–Bellefonte fight was the Elks Club, Miami. While no one truly felt that Robinson would depart the ring as the winner, few if any really felt the fight would be over so quickly. Robinson had been stopped twice before but this was the first time in his career that he had been halted in the first round – proving once again that there's a first time in life for everything.

Sparring Ingemar Johansson

Former world heavyweight champion Ingemar Johansson of Sweden returned to the USA in 1961 for his much-anticipated rematch with Floyd Patterson. The contest against Patterson was due to take place at the Convention Center, Miami Beach. Johansson was bidding to regain the title. Cassius Clay gladly offered his services as a sparring partner to Johansson. While still inexperienced as a professional, Clay gave an exceptionally good account of himself against the former world title holder, which impressed the onlookers in the gym and confirmed the general opinion that the youngster was a little special and had a very bright future ahead of him.

(Note: Johansson failed to regain the title when Patterson knocked him out in round six of fifteen on 13 March 1961.)

Twice in the same month

Donnie Fleeman provided the opposition for Cassius Clay on 21 February 1961. The contest took place at the Auditorium, Miami Beach. Fleeman was no novice to the game, having taken part in forty-seven professional bouts, winning thirty-five and losing eleven, with one drawn. Therefore, it was clear that he knew his business inside the ring. Fleeman was a competitive performer who always came to fight. In his last bout before crossing gloves with Clay, Fleeman had lost a ten-round points decision to Pete Rademacher at the Civic Ice Arena, Seattle, Washington, on 23 January 1961.This was hardly a confidence booster for meeting Clay. However, he was primed and ready to go, with the hope that he might just get a win and in so doing, give his career a boost. Despite his greater experience, Fleeman was no match for Clay, who in his fifth outing kept his undefeated record without being too troubled on the night. Fleeman could not cope with the man in front of him. For Clay it was just another day at the office, or perhaps I should say, another day in the ring. Fleeman was halted in the seventh stanza of a contest set for eight. This was an active time for Clay since this was the first time he had fought twice in the same month.

At first glance

Cassius Clay heard the bell sound to start his sixth professional contest on 19 April 1961 at the Freedom Hall, Louisville. His opponent was LaMar Clark, who entered the ring with a record of forty-five bouts, comprising forty-three wins, with two defeats. During his career, Clark had won twenty-eight of his fights in the opening round, which was impressive. This, of course, suggested that he had power in his mitts. The resume looked a little frightening at first glance and it had to be wondered if Clay's advisors were perhaps a little too ambitious and had miscalculated in making this match against Clark. Were they taking a gamble against an experienced and dangerous puncher? Was this a step too far for the young heavyweight hope? Clark's resume did not really tell the full story. In fact, it more than flattered to deceive. After a closer examination of the respective opponents who had been defeated by Clark, it was more than apparent that they were far from overwhelming opposition and did not have the ring capabilities of Clay, which put a different slant on the match. Therefore, it wasn't likely that Clark would upset the apple cart and be the first to beat Clay.

The last time that Clark had tasted defeat was on 29 June 1960, against Pete Rademacher at Derks Field, Salt Lake City, Utah. Rademacher, an Olympic gold medallist at heavyweight at the 1956 Games, stopped Clark in the tenth and final round of their contest. Before stepping in with Clay, Clark put his name back in the win column when, on 4 March 1961, he knocked out opponent Chuck Wilburn in round two of a scheduled ten. The fight took place at the Convention Center, Las Vegas, Nevada. This was not a win of any great merit but at least Clark emerged from the bout with a victory under his belt, which made him a viable opponent for Clay. The bout against Clark was hardly a demanding one for the man from Louisville and, as expected, he remained undefeated when he knocked out his opponent in the second stanza. The fight was scheduled for eight rounds but clearly from the off it seemed very unlikely that Clark would last the full distance with Clay. Clay was now undefeated in six bouts.

Chapter 3

Fights in Los Angeles

Defeated Apollo Creed's trainer

There was an interesting win on LaMar Clark's boxing record. It was opponent Tony Burton, who, on 4 April 1959, was knocked out in round four in a bout set for the duration of six. The contest took place at the Polo Grounds, Palm Springs, California. It would be true to say that Burton did not create great waves in the sport when participating in the ring. However, after he quit boxing, Burton later found fame in the world of movies when he went on to play the role of Tony Duke Evers, Apollo Creed's trainer, in the Rocky films. Burton retired from boxing with a resume of fourteen fights, of which he won ten and lost three, with one drawn.

Ten rounds for the first time

When Cassius Clay won his contest against Duke Sabedong on points on 26 June 1961, it marked the first occasion in his burgeoning professional career that he had to travel the full distance of ten rounds to gain victory. This was not a bad thing; in fact, it was good experience for the up-and-coming boxer to travel this distance since it tested his stamina.

Sabedong came into the battle zone with a record of twenty-eight bouts, winning fifteen and losing eleven, drawing one, and with one no contest. In his last contest, which had taken place on 2 March 1961, Sabedong fought Alejandro Lavorante at the Olympic Auditorium, Los Angeles, California, and crashed to defeat when knocked out in round five of ten. Sabedong's last victory came on 7 February 1961, when he outpointed Billy Fields over six rounds at the Memorial Auditorium, Sacramento, California. The ever-confident Clay entered the fray against

Sabedong undefeated in six outings and was fully expected to continue his run of victories over his latest opponent. Clay did indeed maintain his perfect record but he was not given an easy ride by Sabedong. The venue for the contest was the Convention Center, Las Vegas.

Going ten rounds for the second time

For the second time in his professional career, Cassius Clay had the experience of being taken the full distance of ten rounds. The venue for the contest was the Freedom Hall, Louisville. The bout took place on 22 July 1961. The opponent was Alonzo Johnson, who had fought on twenty-five occasions in the paid ranks, winning eighteen and losing seven of his bouts. During his time in the ring, Johnson had mixed with many top fighters in the division and had developed into a seasoned performer from the experience of doing so. Before climbing into the ring to exchange punches with Clay, Johnson had lost out in his previous fight when he was outpointed over ten rounds by Alex Miteff at the St Nicholas Arena, New York, on 6 March 1961. The last time Johnson left the ring being victorious was on 15 November the previous year, when he stopped opponent Tony Anthony in round six of a scheduled ten.

The venue for the Johnson–Anthony bout was Palisades Rink, McKeesport, Pennsylvania. It would of course have been better if Johnson had beaten Miteff before going in with Clay. This would have given the fight more appeal. That being said, Johnson was not damaged goods and he didn't arrived in town with the mindset that he was there to lose. In no way did he see himself as fodder for the up-and-coming fighter he was about to square off with. He may have lost his last bout but that didn't mean he was going to lose this one. This was the positive approach Johnson had to take before meeting Clay. However, despite the positive approach, Johnson did lose a points decision at the end of the ten-round contest. Clay defeated him but it was not a runaway victory – far from it. A very ambitious Johnson pushed him hard throughout the fight and gave him a testing time, showing him that professional boxing is a hard game even for a man who had won a gold medal at the Olympic Games. Nothing can be taken for granted once that starting bell rings, even for a budding star. It was notable that Johnson had yet to be stopped or knocked out inside the scheduled distance. This suggested he was a durable fighter – a proud record that he maintained against Clay when he heard the final bell to sound the end of the contest. Clay was now undefeated in eight outings, but Johnson had given him a fight he would long remember.

Argentine opponent

On 7 October 1961, Cassius Clay laced up the gloves once again and met his first Argentine-born opponent in the shape Alex Miteff at the Freedom Hall, Louisville, Kentucky. Miteff was an experienced exponent of the sport having participated in thirty-five bouts, winning twenty-four and losing ten, with one drawn. His last setback in the ring had been on 22 June that year, when he was stopped in round seven in a bout made for ten by Bob Cleroux at the Forum, Montreal, Canada. He got his name back in the win column on 31 August, when, at the Olympic Auditorium, Los Angeles, he knocked out Jimmy McCarter in three rounds of ten.

Miteff was not an easy touch and that was apparent from his record. He always came to do battle and would not surrender easily. He was known to have some sting in his punches, which Clay needed to be cautious of when in the ring with him. Miteff was certainly one tough operator who was always capable of exposing any limitations that his opposition might have. It seemed at the time that Clay might well have a hard night in front of him having to go the full distance to obtain the desired victory, which was important to his career.

When the fight began the spectators sat back in their seats with expectations of watching an entertaining match. What they witnessed came as no disappointment. The Argentine meant business – of that there was no doubt. He landed a solid right hand on Clay's jaw in the second round, which caused a degree of consternation in his corner. This clearly stunned Clay somewhat, yet he was able to shake off the effects of the blow and continue to box. A lesser man might well have ended up on the canvas taking a count from the referee, but Clay stayed on his feet. This was confirmation that he could take a punch, which was encouraging. Even so, Clay did not want to sample too many more of those punches during the bout. He had to avoid the leather bombs that were coming his way. He used his defensive skills and fast footwork to stay out of trouble, but Miteff played the role of the hunter and pursued his prey around the square ring. The fight was close but gradually, Clay started to take control and thus wear his man down, with his hurtful jabs frequently finding their target. Miteff was one tough man but he was in a world of pain and confusion when the fight was finally stopped in the sixth stanza. The bout had been scheduled for ten rounds. Clay's undefeated slate had now reached nine winning fights.

German opponent

Willi Besmanoff became the first German-born boxer to square up to Cassius Clay, which he did on 29 November 1961. The venue once again was the Freedom Hall, Louisville. Besmanoff came with a slate of seventy-eight fights, winning forty-four, losing twenty-seven and drawing seven. It was clear from his resume that he was far from a novice in the sport and had no intention of being a stepping stone for Clay; he had too much pride for that. What could not be ignored when considering Besmanoff's chances in this fight against Clay was the fact that he had lost his last four bouts on the bounce, which suggested he was on the decline and was beatable. Therefore, it was very unlikely that he would pull the rug from under Clay's feet and ruin his perfect record. Besmanoff's last win had taken place on 21 November 1960, when, at the Convention Center, Las Vegas, he boxed his way to a ten-round points victory over Howard King.

The match against Besmanoff was a clever and sensible move for Clay; it was one where he was not only expected to win, but also to look good in doing so. This was an opportunity for him to display his boxing skills to the full, showing the public that he was a man on the way up. Make no mistake, Besmanoff knew his trade and had been around for a long time. He had fought fighters of all styles since the start of his pugilistic career. He had first entered the professional ranks on 15 August 1952 against Heinz Schreiber at the Funkturmhalle, Westend, Berlin. It was not a successful debut for he was knocked out in the fourth and final round of the contest. Besmanoff recovered from that bad start and boxed on, carving out a reputation as a reliable performer. On the night he fought Clay, he was expected to test the Louisville fighter to some degree and give him an argument without being too dangerous. There was always the chance that Besmanoff might get lucky and Clay would underperform. These things do happen in boxing, but not on this occasion.

Besmanoff did not get lucky; in fact, he was far from lucky. He was painfully outclassed from the off. Clay was very much on top form. He meant business: he was sharp, he was fast and he was fully focused on the task in front of him. Besmanoff found his vast experience inside the ring did not help him when up against a man like Clay. He did not have the quality in his boxing skills to come even close to inflicting the first professional defeat on the American's record. Clay was on a very different plane than that of his European opponent. Besmanoff did his best to solve the puzzle in front of him but was unable to do so. Clay was buzzing during the fight, producing all the quality shots, which visibly shook his opponent to the core whenever they landed – and they landed frequently. It soon became very clear that Besmanoff was heading for another defeat on his record. The end finally came when the referee stopped the bout in round seven of a contest set for the duration of ten. Expecting the fight to go the full route was, shall we say, just a little optimistic. Clay left the ring with a tally of ten winning bouts to his credit and his reputation was growing.

Busy period

It is always good for a boxer to stay active and fight at regular intervals. The year 1961 proved to be a busy one for Cassius Clay, who entered the ring and fought on eight occasions. This is the most he would ever box in any one calendar year during his professional career.

Unexpected surprise

Life can be full of surprises; some are good and some are bad. On 10 February 1962 at Madison Square Garden, New York, Sonny Banks gave Cassius Clay and the spectators in attendance an unexpected surprise, or, perhaps, a shock. This came in the shape of a solid left expertly delivered to Clay's chin by Banks. In so doing, Banks wrote his name into the boxing history books by becoming the first man in the professional ranks to floor Clay for a count. This was clearly not in the script. Banks was sending out the message to all and sundry that he was not in the ring just to make up the numbers and come out the loser. He wasn't a sucker; he knew the game and he was going to play it his way, on his terms. He wasn't standing there in front of Clay just for the pay cheque alone; he was there to win – and win big. It wasn't his mission in life to help improve the status of the man he was facing. A victory over Clay would most certainly enhance Banks's reputation. It would soar sky-high, thus opening the doors to more lucrative contests in the future. This thought must have been in the forefront of Banks's mind when he took the bout. How could it not be?

The knockdown took place in the first round, which somewhat shocked Clay, who did not expect to find himself on the canvas at any time during the contest, let alone in the first stanza. At that moment, Banks must have felt that he was on the cusp of scoring a massive win and was on his way to the stars, making headlines on the sports pages. This was Clay's first bout at the Garden and he wanted to look good and impress the New Yorkers with a dazzling performance, showing that he was the genuine article. Being put on the canvas was not a good look for him. This was not the way to impress the fans or convince them that he was a future king of the division. He was up quickly but had to take the mandatory eight count from the referee. Clay now realised that the man sharing the ring with him was not to be taken lightly; he meant business and had to be taken care of sooner rather than later.

Banks had entered the ring to face Clay with a record comprising twelve bouts, winning ten and losing two. The last time he had lost a contest was on 6 February 1961, when at the Marigold Gardens in Chicago, Illinois, he lost a five-round points decision to Chuck Garrett. He recovered from that defeat and bounced back with five wins. One of these included his last outing against Clay Thomas on 27 January 1962, whom he stopped in the second stanza of a ten-round contest at the Graystone Ballroom, Detroit, Michigan.

The knockdown by Banks fired up Clay, who quickly got down to work and returned the compliment with interest when he put his opponent down for a count in round two. Many were aware that this was the beginning of the end for Banks. Clay continued to increase his work rate, putting his punches together and eventually taking his undefeated record to eleven when he brought the fight to a close, stopping his opponent in the fourth round in a contest schedule for ten. Now the knock-down by Banks may well have been a blow to Clay's ego but it also revealed his character as a fighter with him being able to recover and win the bout in style.

Ruby Goldstein

When Ruby Goldstein stepped into the ring at Madison Square Garden in New York to officiate the Clay–Banks fight, he didn't realise that he was fated to become the first referee to count over Clay in the professional ranks.

Twice in a month for a second time

Cassius Clay pulled on the gloves once more on 28 February 1962 at the Convention Center, Miami Beach in Florida, where he got down to business on meeting his opponent, Don Warner. The fighter facing Clay had graced the ring on twenty occasions, winning twelve, losing six and drawing two. Warner was a puncher who had put away eleven of his opponents inside the scheduled distance. This looked impressive – something for Clay and his management team to be aware of. There are, however, levels in boxing, and when taking a detailed look at the men whom Warner had beaten before the final bell, it was noticeable that they were not exactly world-beaters. This, in turn, indicated that the man from Louisville would not be in any real danger of losing this contest. But Clay knew he could not afford to be complacent with regards to the man he was facing.

Warner was from Philadelphia, Pennsylvania, a city with a reputation for turning out a number of tough fighters who were unyielding in battle. Clay had learnt a stern lesson in his last fight against Sonny Banks when floored for a count in the opening round: every opponent faced inside the ring is a threat and that threat should not be underestimated – to do so could prove catastrophic. The last man to have beaten Warner was Billy Daniels, who stopped him in round three in a contest set for ten on 11 December 1961. The Daniels–Warner fight took place at St Nicholas

Arena, New York. Then, on 1 February 1962, Warner got back on the winning trail when he scored a victory by making short work of Orie Paschall, whom he stopped in the first stanza of a contest planned for ten. The venue for that contest was the Blue Horizon, Philadelphia. At the time of his bout with Warner, Clay was undefeated in eleven contests and was moving steadily in the rankings in an upwards direction.

The success continued when Clay maintained a perfect resume by stopping Warner in round four of ten. From the moment the first bell rang to start the action, Clay quickly got down to work and it soon became apparent which fighter was going to finish second in this bout. You did not need to be Nostradamus or indeed a boxing expert to know that it wasn't going to be Clay – not by a long shot. Warner was soon in deep water and sinking fast against Clay. There was no lifeguard on hand to save him, only the referee, who acted in the same capacity and saved him by halting the proceedings at the right time. Warner, to his credit, was game, but just being game does not win fights. From the start, Warner was at a loss to know how to compete with the man with whom he was sharing the ring. Clay was too fast and too skilful for him, constantly scoring with his punishing left jab, which he used with deadly precision.

Clay was keeping very busy; this contest marked the second time he had fought fight twice in the same month.

Debut in Los Angeles

Cassius Clay had his first professional outing in Los Angeles on 23 April 1962 at the Sports Arena. He arrived in the city of angels sporting an undefeated record of twelve contests – and had every intention of keeping his perfect record intact. Clay wanted all to know they were watching a boxing genius and a world heavyweight champion of the future; they should sit back and savour every second of the moment he was in action. While Clay was talented and considered a hot prospect, he was still new where professional boxing was concerned. There was still some way for him to go before he would be knocking at the door of the reigning world champion. At this stage of his career, many critics were cautious about his long-term prospects.

Fights in Los Angeles

A number of highly touted fighters in the past had shown talent and looked to be heading for the top, only to fall at the final hurdle. In some cases, they didn't even make it to the final hurdle. It was hoped that Clay was not going join the ranks of hopefuls who failed when put to the test. For Clay, at that moment in his career, it was a case of so far so good. George Logan was the opponent who came into the ring to face Clay. He brought with him a record of thirty-two fights, winning twenty-four, losing seven and drawing one. In his last contest, which had taken place on 5 March 1962, Logan had been defeated by Canadian Bob Cleroux by way of a seventh-round stoppage in a scheduled ten. The battleground for the Logan–Cleroux fight had been the Civic Auditorium, San Francisco, California. The loss against Cleroux did not bode well for Logan's chances with Clay. Anyone who studied the sport closely knew that Logan would be lucky to hear the final bell. Logan knew what he was up against but he was not intimidated by Clay, which was admirable when considering the growing reputation of the man he was about to face.

It was not a challenging night for Clay; he did not get out of first gear during the contest. To be truthful, he really didn't need to. If Logan had a game plan, it wasn't working. Logan was outclassed, and was stopped in the fourth round of a bout scheduled for ten. To his credit, Logan pushed forward, attempting to land a telling punch on his opponent – a punch that would upset the odds – but that was easier said than done when up against a fighter like Clay. At no time did Logan ever look like being a potential roadblock to the progress of the man from Louisville. Clay showed his ring superiority throughout the bout, moving well, boxing in a classy way and confirming his potential. It was onwards and upwards for the undefeated prospect.

Chapter 4

Clay Beats Cooper

Battle of the undefeated

On 19 May 1962, Cassius Clay faced his first professional opponent with an undefeated record. His name was Billy Daniels, a fighter who stepped into the ring having won all sixteen of his previous bouts. Daniels also had his dreams of making it to the top in boxing. Clay came into the bout also undefeated in his previous thirteen fights.

This looked like being a testing contest for the man from Louisville. In his previous bout before meeting Clay, Daniels had outpointed Claude Chapman over ten rounds. This was not a challenging fight for Daniels but one that kept him ticking over, keeping him active and sharp. The Daniels–Chapman contest had taken place on 29 January 1962 at the same venue where Daniels was now to meet Clay – the St Nicholas Arena, New York. Daniels had fought here eight times previously so he felt very much at home, and must have hoped that his winning streak at the arena would continue. Both boxers were obviously keen to maintain their undefeated slate and thus go on to bigger and better fights. So there was a great deal to play for in this bout – the stakes were high. It is always an exciting prospect when two fighters meet who have yet to have a loss on their record. It adds a little more spice to the action, giving it that much more appeal.

Daniels was no mug. He knew that a win over Clay would make him a major name in the division – a name that would make him a most sought-after fighter, adding a few more noughts on the end of the pay cheque for his next fight. This clearly bolstered Daniels' incentive to gain victory in the bout. Clay also knew that he had to win to ensure his journey to the top continued – not just win, but to win in an impressive, eye-catching style. This would encourage the public to talk about his talent with the conviction that he was going to be the next world champion when the opportunity came his way.

The fight was not a walkover for Clay; he had to dig deep in his effort to come out on top. As expected, Daniels was one tough cookie, with boxing skills to be respected, and hence gave Clay a hard fight. Daniels was not going to roll over easily in this bout; he was determined to leave the ring victorious. However, Clay kept his unblemished record intact when he stopped Daniels with a cut eye in round seven of the scheduled ten.

Still undefeated

Cassius Clay was back inside the ring on 20 July 1962, facing his second Argentine opponent in the shape of Alejandro Lavorante. The contest took place at the Sports Arena, Los Angeles. Lavorante was not an easy man to fight; he knew what the gloved game was all about. He was not likely be overwhelmed or impressed by the reputation of the man he was about to face.

Lavorante entered the bout with a record of twenty-two fights, with nineteen victories and three defeats. His standout win had taken place on 11 May 1961 in Los Angeles, the venue for the bout being the Olympic Auditorium, where he had knocked out the highly regarded Zora Folley in round seven. The fight had been set for the duration of ten rounds. The win over Folley served as a warning for Clay that the man he was facing could be dangerous and should not be taken lightly. Certainly you could not go to sleep in the ring when confronting a fighter like Lavorante. If you did, he was more than capable of putting you to sleep on the canvas with the referee counting over you. You had to stay alert, not let your concentration wander for one split second.

It was felt that Lavorante would certainly come out with all guns firing once the bell had sounded to start the fight. The man from Argentina had everything to gain and nothing to lose in this meeting. The rewards for beating Clay would be immense, so to some extent, Lavorante could afford to throw caution to the wind and go for broke. Before stepping through the ropes to engage Clay, Lavorante had lost his previous contest to former world light-heavyweight king Archie Moore, on 30 March 1962, when stopped in the tenth and final round at the Sports Arena, Los Angeles.

Clay was as confident as ever that he would add another defeat to his opponent's record and leave the ring victorious. At no time did he contemplate losing to Lavorante – the thought never entered his mind. Based on his previous outings to date, you could not argue with his prediction of the outcome of the fight. True to form, Clay turned it on and added to his win column and reputation by knocking out Lavorante in the fifth stanza of a scheduled ten. The man from Louisville was now undefeated in fifteen professional fights and was looking better in each outing.

Opponent with the most professional contests

It was time for Cassius Clay to go into action again, and in his sixteenth professional contest, in scintillating form he added to his undefeated record when he stopped former world light-heavyweight champion Archie Moore in round four of twelve. The bout took place on 15 November 1962 at the Sports Arena, Los Angeles. At the time of the contest, Moore had a professional record of 218 fights, winning 185, losing twenty-two and drawing ten, with one no contest. Moore's resume read like a *Who's Who* of boxing – you name him, he'd fought him. Never again in his career would Clay face a professional opponent who had participated in the number of bouts that Moore had. Without a doubt, Moore was considered one of the greats in the light-heavyweight division.

Moore and Clay were not exactly strangers to each other. The former light-heavyweight king had been Clay's trainer in the early stages of his professional career before Angelo Dundee eventually took over the role. This added a little intrigue to the fight. Clay was expected to secure the victory over Moore, who now had a number of miles on the clock and was showing signs of wear and tear. This wasn't surprising. Moore had been around for a long time and had indulged in some very tough and high-profile fights inside the ring along the way. However, there was this lingering question of whether the former trainer would know a little too much for his one-time student and spring a surprise in the bout. It would be true to say that Moore knew all the tricks of the trade and what he didn't know simply wasn't worth knowing. There was little Moore hadn't seen before in a sport that he had served so well and successfully. In his previous contest, on 28 May 1962, Moore had drawn over ten rounds with future world light-heavyweight champion Willie Pastrano at the LA Sports Arena. This was not a bad result at all since it showed that, even in his later years, he still had the skills with which to trouble the best. Moore, nicknamed the Old Mongoose, had some fire left in his fighting soul and was determined not to give Clay an easy night.

Prior to the contest with Moore, Clay was as confident as ever that he would emerge victorious. He could not see any way in which Moore would be able to defeat him. His confidence was well founded: the hot prospect was getting hotter in each bout he contested. It was evident that it would take someone special to beat Clay.

Challenged twice for the world heavyweight title

Archie Moore, while an outstanding world light-heavyweight king, was no stranger to the heavyweight poundage. Moore had in the past mixed with good company in the division. This included seeing him challenge twice for the world heavyweight title. The first was against Rocky Marciano on 21 September 1955, making a bright start when dropping the champion for a count in the second stanza. Marciano recovered and knocked out Moore in round nine of a scheduled fifteen. The contest took place at the Yankee Stadium, Bronx, New York. The second attempt took place on 30 November 1956, when competing for the vacant crown against Floyd Patterson following the retirement of Marciano from the sport. Moore was knocked out in round five of fifteen at the Chicago Stadium in Illinois.

Requiem for a heavyweight

There have been a number of boxing films produced over the years. Some good and some, in all truth, not so good. In 1962, a film was made about the sport that could be added to the category of 'good': *Requiem for a Heavyweight*, which starred Anthony Quinn in the lead role as Luis Mountain Rivera. Also in the main cast were Jackie Gleason, Mickey Rooney and Julie Harris. Quinn, as one would expect from an actor of his class, gave an outstanding and heartfelt performance of a boxer who was going nowhere in his fighting career. The film added some realism to the story when it also included Cassius Clay in the cast, who appeared as himself in a punishing boxing scene with Rivera.

Inside the distance wins

Charlie Powell was the next opponent to go head to head with Cassius Clay, on 24 January 1963. The likelihood of him winning was a little remote, to say the least. Stylistically, Powell was made to order for Clay. True to expectations, a victory was never within Powell's reach while the bout lasted, try as he might. The gulf in class was way too wide for Powell to bridge. He was exchanging punches with a boxing master who was always getting the better of him. Clay read his opponent's moves perfectly. Powell's night of boxing came to an end when he was knocked out in the third round of a slated ten.

Powell was not exactly a newcomer to the sport. He had entered the ring against Clay with a record of thirty-two professional bouts, winning twenty-three, losing six and drawing three. Powell was last defeated on 3 July 1962 by John Riggins when stopped in the third of a scheduled ten rounds at the Auditorium, Oakland, California. Powell punched his way back into the win column in his previous bout before meeting Clay. He accomplished this when he outpointed Dave Furch at the Olympic Auditorium, Los Angeles, on 1 November 1962.

The Clay–Powell contest took place at the Civic Arena, Pittsburgh, Pennsylvania. Clay was now undefeated in seventeen bouts. Up to this point in time, he had fought a number of good fighters on his journey through the heavyweight division but no one who represented a real danger to him. To be fair, no one would have truthfully expected Clay to go in with world-rated opposition at this early stage. That would have been somewhat foolish, since Clay would have been involved in punishing, hard-fought battles that would have shortened his boxing career. Based on his performances to date, it was now obviously time for Clay to move up in class – time to step into the ring and mix with more demanding opposition. This would enhance his ring education and put him in good stead for the big challenges that would surely come in the future.

A world heavyweight title was looming on the horizon. He just had to continue notching up impressive victories to ensure he got the chance. The win over Powell provided Clay with his longest ever run of successive inside the distance victories, which now stood at nine in a row.

Clay Beats Cooper

First sell-out

On 13 March 1963, Cassius Clay entered the ring to confront his latest opponent, Doug Jones. The contest took place at Madison Square Garden, New York. Clay, now undefeated in seventeen bouts, was favoured to win and maintain his perfect record. It was clear that Jones was not a fighter who would surrender and consider that he was fated to lose this bout – far from it. He entered the fray with a resume of twenty-five fights, winning twenty-one and losing three, with one drawn. Jones had taken part in his first professional bout on 22 August 1958, winning a four-round points decision over his opponent, Jimmy McNair, at Madison Square Garden. From that point on, he engaged in a number of bouts that helped to cultivate his ring skills. The high point for Jones came on 12 May 1962, when he challenged Harold Johnson for the NBA and vacant NYSAC world light-heavyweight crown at the Philadelphia Arena, Pennsylvania, where he lost a fifteen-round points decision. This was in no way a disgrace; Johnson was a class operator, a smart fighter who had the kind of ring craft lauded by many who follow the sport.

When looking at the situation realistically it was clear that Clay held no fears for Jones, who was used to taking part in big fights against major names in the sport. Prior to meeting Clay, Jones had won his last two bouts in impressive style, stopping future world light-heavyweight king Bob Foster in eight rounds of ten on 20 October 1962. Then, on 15 December 1962, Zora Folley failed to last the ten-round distance when knocked out in round seven. Both fights had taken place at Madison Square Garden. Jones had fought twelve times in total at the Garden and he was yet to lose at this venue. Was this a good omen for him? It was apparent that Clay could not take anything for granted against this opponent. Only a foolish man underestimates his opposition in the ring, and the man from Louisville was no fool. No one could ever pin that label on him. Clay was aware that he could not lose his focus against an opponent who was more than capable of springing an upset if given the opportunity. A loss here would undo all the previous hard work Clay had put in to reach this point. He knew he could not afford to slip up. Jones wasn't going to give Clay a free pass in this contest. He intended to take him to places he had not been to before in the ring. Clay had tasted the highs of victory but Jones was confident that he would introduce him to the lows of defeat. Jones wanted the win and wanted it badly.

On the night, Jones pulled out all the stops in his efforts to gain victory over Clay. The fight went the full route of ten rounds. During the fast-paced battle, Jones methodically went about his work and showed no indication that he would quit. He was determined to end his opponent's unbeaten run and in so doing, bolster his own future. To say Jones gave Clay various problems in the fight would be an understatement. It was by no means one-way traffic for the ex-Olympic gold medallist. Clay had to battle hard to ensure he kept his undefeated slate. Jones would often score with eye-catching flurries. At the final bell, Clay's weary hand was raised in victory. Jones was disappointed at the result since he felt he had done enough during the fight to get the decision. However, he came out of the contest with a good deal of credit. In fact, his stock in the boxing world had risen considerably after giving the hot prospect a hard and close bout. Some who witnessed the fight indeed felt that Jones was unlucky not to have been given the decision. Such was the appeal of the match, it was later reported that the Clay–Jones contest had been a box-office winner, giving Madison Square Garden its first sell-out in thirteen years.

Jones secures WBA world heavyweight title shot

The loss to Cassius Clay did not deter or dampen the hopes of Doug Jones in his attempt to become a world heavyweight champion. The ambition was still burning bright within him to obtain a version of the crown. Jones fought on, winning eight of his next ten bouts. On 28 June 1966, at the Sam Houston Coliseum, Houston, Texas, Jones secured a world title shot and challenged the then reigning WBA king, Ernie Terrell, a fighter who had compiled a record of forty-two bouts, winning thirty-eight and losing four. Jones felt he had the skills to topple the champion and take the title but came up empty when he lost a fifteen-round points decision to Terrell. This put an end to any aspirations that Jones may have had of one day becoming a world heavyweight champion.

After the Terrell bout, Jones went on to fight on four occasions, winning just one of the respected bouts. This indicated that Jones had reached the end of the road. One of the fighters who defeated Jones was future world heavyweight king Joe Frazier, who knocked him out in round six of ten on 21 February 1967. The venue for the Frazier–Jones bout was the Philadelphia Arena.

Outside of the USA

Cassius Clay took part in his first professional contest outside of the USA on 18 June 1963 at Wembley Stadium, London. It is, without a shadow of a doubt, risky for a fighter to box in another country since this requires him to meet an opponent on his own turf. The said risk is obvious: all the advantages are with the local man and the decision in a close fight often goes to the home fighter. At the time, Clay was widely regarded as a fighter on his way to the top – a world champion in waiting. His opponent was the reigning British and Commonwealth heavyweight champion Henry Cooper. The British fighter had good credentials but was not considered a serious threat to the progress of the American.

The team behind Clay were not going to risk his undefeated record at this stage and destroy all the previous hard work. They were too close to their target – the fearsome Sonny Liston, the reigning world heavyweight king. They would have researched the British fighter thoroughly and considered him a safe bet, a sure-fire win for their man. Cooper was merely there to make Clay look good and thus add to the American's growing reputation – or so it was thought at the time.

The Briton was no soft touch; he had been around a long time in the game. Cooper had made his professional debut on 14 September 1954, knocking out opponent Harry Painter in round one of six at the Harringay Arena in London. This was a dream start for the London-born fighter, who in the years to follow became a force to be reckoned with on the domestic and Europe front. Before meeting Clay, Cooper had fought on 26 March 1963 at the Empire Pool, Wembley, London. That night, Cooper retained his British and Commonwealth crown against former European heavyweight king Dick Richardson by a five-round knockout in a scheduled fifteen.

Cooper was a no-nonsense type of fighter who was well schooled in the art of boxing, and the American was not going to intimidate him in any way. The British fighter had seen it all before. To Cooper, Clay was just another opponent – perhaps a little special, but at the end of the day he was human and as such he could be hurt if hit, and Cooper could certainly hit, there was no doubt about that. The Briton's famed left hook, known as 'Enry's 'Ammer, was a fearsome weapon that had put paid to many an opponent who had shared the ring with him over the years. It was very foolish for anyone to sell Cooper short or even expose their chin to him during a fight. Consequently, Clay found out painfully that the reputation of Cooper's punch was not exaggerated in any way whatsoever. It was indeed a lethal weapon – one to both respect and fear. Prior to the contest with Cooper, Clay had predicted that he would win easily inside the distance.

When the fight got underway, the American danced around the ring, shooting out his left jab into Cooper's face. The aggressive Briton started quickly, cutting down the ring, attacking his opponent without hesitation and bringing blood from Clay's nose. The spectators loved what they were seeing and cheered loudly the British fighter for his early success. Cooper meant business and was looking for the knockout; he wanted to take the American out in style. The second session was much the same as the first one, this time ending with Cooper cut under the left eye. This was not good news for the Brit.

The later rounds slipped by without any real drama. The two men were looking for the opening that just might win them the bout. They continued to exchange left jabs, with the home fans hoping this would be Cooper's night and he would somehow find the finishing punch to put the arrogant fighter from the USA away for an historic win. A victory over Clay would put Cooper and British boxing on the map, big time. Then, in round four, the Briton's explosive left hook found its target. Clay slid down the ropes and came to rest on the canvas. Cooper at that moment became just the second man in the professional ranks to put him on the deck (the first fighter to have done so being American Sonny Banks on 10 February 1962 at Madison Square Garden). The excited fans felt a victory was in sight for their man. Alarm bells must have been ringing loudly in Clay's corner. This was an unexpected turn of events; this was not supposed to happen; this was not part of the plan. Had they sold Cooper short, much to the detriment of their man? Clay was supposed to win at a canter, show his skills and then return home with another win on his record. The British fighter was dangerous – a fact the visitor from the USA and his corner team were now more than aware of. Clay was clearly shaken by Cooper and looked ready for the taking. The blood pressure of many of the fans must have risen highly with their anticipation of a Cooper victory. Fortunately for Clay, the bell sounded to end the session before the home fighter could capitalise on his success and potentially produce the upset of the year. Clay had time to recover in his corner and came out for the next round refreshed and very switched on, ending the session in round five of the scheduled ten. The finish came due to a bad cut over Cooper's left eye. The blood ran freely down his face, staining the canvas beneath his feet. The referee had no alternative but to stop the bout. This had been a close call for Clay – too close for comfort. At the time of their meeting, Clay was undefeated in eighteen bouts whilst Cooper had a tally of thirty-six fights with twenty-seven wins and eight defeats, with one draw.

The London Palladium

The Cassius Clay–Henry Cooper fight was a big deal in the UK and it sparked a great deal of interest amongst the public. Even the non-boxing fans were curious about this cocky, arrogant American who was going up against our 'Enry. It really was a major talking point. The weigh-in for the two fighters took place on the stage at the London Palladium, a renowned theatre that had, over the years, seen many international stars from all over the world perform.

How to make an entrance

Cassius Clay always had a creative flare, a knack of attracting attention – a talent he possessed in addition to his obvious boxing skills. He knew how to sell a fight, how to turn the ordinary into the extraordinary. The world was changing fast and he realised that fighters and the world of boxing also had to change. A boxer could not simply turn up to fight any more; he also had to entertain if he was to be noticed by the media. In his ring walk when meeting Henry Cooper, Clay once again showed his innovation skills. He wasn't going to just walk into the ring in the standard fashion. He was going to do something different. He entered the ring wearing a crown and an eye-catching red and white gown with the words 'Cassius Clay The Greatest' emblazoned on the back.

Chapter 5

Shocks the World

The prediction

Fortune-tellers often reveal what the future holds for those who wish to know. Cassius Clay was not a fortune-teller but he did make a habit of predicting the future of many fighters he was about to face. He would, with all confidence, predict the round in which he would defeat his opponents prior to their contest. More often than not, his forecast would come true. He predicted that he would defeat Henry Cooper in the fifth round – which of course, to the dismay of the many Cooper fans, he did.

Jack Solomons

Jack Solomons promoted the Cassius Clay–Henry Cooper contest and in so doing became the first to bring the highly regarded boxer from the USA to British shores. Solomons had been around the fight scene for a number of years and was thus an experienced and well-respected man in the world of boxing – a true legend.

Tommy, the first

When Cassius Clay fought Henry Cooper, Londoner Tommy Little – an experienced ring official – became the first British referee to handle a contest involving the boxer from the USA. His name may have been 'little' but he was more than big enough to handle the bout between the two heavyweights.

First Briton

When Henry Cooper fought Cassius Clay on 18 June 1963 at Wembley Stadium, he became the first British-born fighter to cross gloves with the highly touted ex-gold medallist in the professional ranks. At the time that may not have seemed that much of a big deal but later developments confirmed that this was indeed a special occasion.

Only European boxer

Henry Cooper became the only boxer from Europe to have sent Cassius Clay to the canvas for a count during his professional career. When considering what the USA-born fighter later went on to achieve during his outstanding career and the hard punchers he faced, that really was some feat by the British boxer.

Gorgeous George

George Raymond Wagner was born on 24 March 1915 in Butte, Nebraska, USA. In later years, he took up the sport of wrestling and became a major attraction – a character who caught the attention of sports fans. He fought under the name of Gorgeous George. Cassius Clay acknowledged that he copied the boastful style that George would often display before his bouts to promote the fight and draw in the spectators. George died on 26 December 1963.

The Beatles

On 18 February 1964, while in training for his world heavyweight title shot at Sonny Liston, Cassius Clay was paid a surprise visit by the British pop sensation The Beatles. The group called in at the 5th St. Gym in Miami Beach, Florida. Both The Beatles and Clay were destined to make history on a large scale in their chosen professions.

Muhammad Ali: The Man Who Changed Boxing

Corner retirement

On 25 February 1964, Cassius Clay confounded many critics when he won the world heavyweight title from the defending champion, Sonny Liston, who retired in his corner in round six of a scheduled fifteen. Liston retired from the contest due to a shoulder injury that prevented him from carrying on. The contest took place at the Convention Center, Miami Beach. Prior to the fight, the challenger had taunted the champion constantly with numerous insults, which clearly annoyed him. No one had ever disrespected Liston like this before. At the time, it seemed foolish for Clay to employ such a tactic against the fearsome title holder. It was akin to poking a hornet's nest with a stick and then standing in front of it waiting for a reaction – a reaction that one knew, based on the knowledge of the hornet, would not be a happy one. It has to be wondered if Clay was walking a dangerous road, one leading him to certain disaster, or had he seen a weakness in Liston that no one else had? Liston was a powerful and frightening fighter who took no prisoners inside the ring. He was always looking to land the finishing punch to end the fight before the final bell. 'Seek and destroy' appeared to be his mantra, especially where his latest challenger was concerned. It seemed that Liston was going to take great delight in pulling this young upstart apart by giving him a beating for the many insults that he had endured leading up to the fight.

Clay, who was very much the underdog, entered the fray with an undefeated record of nineteen bouts. The wise men, the hardened experts of boxing who had been around the game for years, gave Clay little chance of taking Liston down. It was a boy against a man – a delusional boy who was going to be given a painful lesson in what boxing was all about by the defending title holder. Liston had met and beaten better opposition than his challenger had during his time in the ring, which begged the question, what could Clay bring to the party that Liston had not already seen before? It seemed Clay had a mountain to climb against the tough champion – one that looked like he would be unable to ascend successfully.

It appeared that Clay would no longer have an undefeated record after Liston had stoically taken care of business. Clay was a talented boxer, of that there was no doubt. Had he been going in with another fighter holding the crown he might well have had a good chance of winning the title. Liston had a slate of thirty-six fights, winning thirty-five of them, with twenty-five of them ending inside the scheduled distance, and just the one defeat. Even with the best will in the world, it really seemed most unlikely prior to the bout that Clay would inflict the second loss on Liston's record.

Liston made his professional debut on 2 September 1953 at the Arena, Saint Louis, Missouri, where he made short work of opponent Don Smith, stopping him in the first round of four. From that moment on, Liston worked his way to the top of the tree and looked set to remain there for a very long time. So in the aftermath of the fight, Clay could afford to be a little smug since he more than proved the many doubters wrong in obtaining his victory. Clay showed that he could back up his words with his boxing ability and he was for real. During the contest, Liston looked, at times, to be a little frustrated. He was not able to get to grips with the fast-moving opponent who jabbed and moved until the end came.

Light-heavyweight gold medallist

By defeating Sonny Liston, Cassius Clay became the first Olympic gold medallist at the light-heavyweight poundage to win the world heavyweight title in the professional ranks.

Angelo Dundee saves the day

When challenging Sonny Liston for the world heavyweight title, Cassius Clay claimed that during the fourth round a substance had found its way into his eyes. This hindered Clay's sight badly, which put him in danger of getting caught by one of Liston's heavy punches, thus ending his bid for the crown. However, when he returned to his corner, trainer Angelo Dundee didn't panic; he stayed calm and cleaned Clay's eyes. When the bell sounded to resume the action, Dundee sent his charge out for the fifth stanza. Clay's eyes eventually cleared and he was able to take control of the contest from there on in, scoring an astonishing win to add the world title to his name. Without the wisdom and fight corner experience of Dundee, the outcome may well have been different.

Chapter 6

Another World Heavyweight Title Bout in the USA

The fifth boxer

When Cassius Clay defeated Sonny Liston to win the world heavyweight crown he became just the fifth boxer to win the title with an undefeated record. The previous fighters who could claim they had won the championship with an unbeaten resume were pugilists like James J. Corbett, James J. Jeffries, Rocky Marciano and Ingemar Johansson. (John L. Sullivan was undefeated when he captured the heavyweight championship but he is not included on the respected list since he won the title under the London Prize Ring rules.)

The twenty-third world champion

When taking the world heavyweight title from Sonny Liston, Cassius Clay became the twenty-third boxer to win the title. The previous holders of the heavyweight crown were: James J. Corbett, Bob Fitzsimmons, James J. Jeffries, Marvin Hart, Tommy Burns, Jack Johnson, Jess Willard, Jack Dempsey, Gene Tunney, Max Schmeling, Jack Sharkey, Primo Carnera, Max Baer, James J. Braddock, Joe Louis, Ezzard Charles, Jersey Joe Walcott, Lee Savold, Rocky Marciano, Floyd Patterson, Ingemar Johansson and Sonny Liston. (John L. Sullivan has been omitted from the list since he was a world champion under London Prize Ring rules.)

The eighteenth USA-born world heavyweight title holder

When Cassius Clay won the world heavyweight title, he became the eighteenth USA-born boxer to win championship. Of previous champions, Bob Fitzsimmons was British, Tommy Burns was Canadian, Max Schmeling was German, Primo Carnera was Italian and Ingemar Johannson was Swedish.

One hundred and sixth

The Cassius Clay–Sonny Liston encounter was the 106th world heavyweight title contest to have taken place. That figure starts from the James J. Corbett–John L. Sullivan championship bout, which is regarded as the first heavyweight title fought under the modern rules. The historical Corbett–Sullivan contest took place on 7 September 1892, the venue being the Olympic Club in New Orleans, Louisiana. Corbett won the championship when he knocked out Sullivan in round twenty-one in a fight to the finish.

The ninety-second world heavyweight title contest

It was not unusual to see world heavyweight title fights staged in the USA. The Cassius Clay–Sonny Liston bout followed the tradition and became the ninety-second world heavyweight title contest to have been staged in that country. Fourteen previous bouts had taken place in other parts of the world: England (three times), Ireland (once), France (four times), Australia (three times), Cuba (once), Canada (once), and Italy (once).

The eighteenth boxer

When Cassius Clay defeated Sonny Liston to win the world heavyweight championship he became the eighteenth boxer to do so by taking the title inside the scheduled distance. This also includes winning the title by way of a disqualification. The other fighters who won the crown before the final bell are: James J. Corbett, Bob Fitzsimmons, James J. Jeffries, Marvin Hart, Jack Johnson, Jess Willard, Jack Dempsey, Max Schmeling, Primo Carnera, Max Baer, Joe Louis, Jersey Joe Walcott, Lee Savold, Rocky Marciano, Floyd Patterson, Ingemar Johansson and Sonny Liston.

The seventh world heavyweight champion

In winning the world heavyweight crown, Cassius Clay became just the seventh black boxer to do so. Previous black winners were: Jack Johnson, Joe Louis, Ezzard Charles, Jersey Joe Walcott, Floyd Patterson and Sonny Liston.

Sonny Liston's first professional defeat

Prior to his defeat to Cassius Clay, during his professional career Sonny Liston had only once been beaten inside the square ring. The opponent who defeated Liston was Marty Marshall, who outpointed him over eight rounds on 7 September 1954 at the Motor City Arena, Detroit, Michigan. Marshall's win over Liston was not expected; it was something of a shock – a minor one, true, but a shock nevertheless. Prior to the bout it looked like Liston would be too much for his opponent. However, these things happen in boxing: always expect the unexpected when heavyweights collide in the ring. The big boys are known to spring a surprise from time to time.

Liston gained sweet revenge over Marshall on 21 April 1955, when he stepped into the ring at the Kiel Auditorium, Saint Louis in Missouri. Liston put matters right when he stopped Marshall in round six of a scheduled eight. The two fighters renewed hostilities for the third time on 6 March 1956, the venue on this occasion being the Duquesne Gardens in Pittsburgh, Pennsylvania. Liston put any doubts to rest on who was the better fighter of the two when he defeated Marshall on points over the duration of ten rounds.

First man to stop Sonny Liston

Cassius Clay not only won the world heavyweight championship when he defeated Sonny Liston, he also became the first man in the professional ranks to stop him inside the scheduled distance. That was some achievement by Clay – especially when you consider the number of fights in which Liston had participated against a number of top-class fighters, many of whom were big punchers in their own right.

Another World Heavyweight Title Bout in the USA

Barney Felix

Barney Felix was the referee in charge of the Sonny Liston–Cassius Clay bout. This was the second world heavyweight championship contest in which Felix was the third man in the ring. On 15 August 1950, he refereed the world heavyweight title contest that saw Ezzard Charles successfully defend his NBA version of the crown by stopping his challenger, Freddie Beshore, in round fourteen in a contest set for the duration of fifteen. The venue for the Charles–Beshore fight was the Memorial Auditorium, Buffalo, New York.

The first judges

Whilst Barney Felix became the first man to referee a world heavyweight title bout involving Cassius Clay, the distinction of being the first judges to reside at a world championship contest that saw Clay in action fell to Gus Jacobson and Bunny Lovett.

Chapter 7

A New Name

Dundee and McDonald

Chris Dundee and Bill McDonald promoted the Cassius Clay–Sonny Liston contest. By doing so, they became the first to promote a world heavyweight title fight that involved Clay. (Chris Dundee was the older brother of Angelo Dundee.)

First since Jess Willard

When Sonny Liston lost his title to Cassius Clay by retiring in his corner, he became the first defending world heavyweight champion to do so since Jess Willard. Willard lost his world crown to Jack Dempsey on 4 July 1919, when he retired in the third stanza of twelve in a contest that took place at the Bay View Park Arena, Toledo, Ohio.

A young champion

When Cassius Clay defeated Sonny Liston to win the world heavyweight crown, he created a record by becoming the youngest fighter at the time to win the championship from the reigning title holder. Clay at the time was 22 years, 1 month and 8 days old. It would be true to say that Floyd Patterson won the crown at a younger age than Clay, having been 21 years, 10 months and 26 days, but he did so by winning the vacant crown when contesting it against Archie Moore on 30 November 1956 and not from a defending champion.

A New Name

Mike Tyson beats Clay and Patterson's record

It is often said that records are made to be broken. Mike Tyson more than confirmed this when he beat both Floyd Patterson and Muhammad Ali's respective records of being the youngest fighter to win the world heavyweight crown. On 22 November 1986, a new record was indeed created in a contest that took place at the Hilton Hotel, Las Vegas. At the age of 20 years, 4 months and 23 days. The hard-punching Tyson destroyed the then WBC heavyweight king Trevor Berbick in a painful two rounds to win the title. Tyson was the firm favourite to take the crown prior to the contest. While the bout was set for twelve rounds, it was clear from the sound of the first bell that the fight would not go the scheduled distance and would end with a new title holder being crowned when the dust had settled.

Second gold medallist to win the heavyweight championship of the world

When Cassius Clay defeated Sonny Liston to win the world heavyweight title he became just the second Olympic gold medallist to achieve it. The first boxer to do so was Floyd Patterson, who captured the vacant crown on 30 November 1956, following the retirement of Rocky Marciano. Patterson on that occasion knocked out Archie Moore in the fifth stanza in a bout scheduled for fifteen rounds. The contest was staged at the Chicago Stadium, Illinois. Patterson won the gold medal in the middleweight division at the Helsinki Games in Finland in 1952, where he secured the medal in spectacular fashion by knocking out his opponent, Vasile Tiţă of Romania, in the opening round of the contest.

Won and lost

Sonny Liston became the first boxer in the history of the sport to win the world heavyweight championship from one former Olympic gold medallist (Floyd Patterson) and then, in turn, lose the title to another former Olympic gold medallist (Cassius Clay).

Muhammad Ali: The Man Who Changed Boxing

Clay the vocalist

Many boxers have had a crack at singing over the years and Cassius Clay was no exception. In 1964, he released a record of him singing the Ben E. King classic *Stand By Me* and surprised many by proving to be a good vocalist. The man could blast out a song as well as blasting out opponents in the ring.

Name change

Soon after defeating Sonny Liston, Cassius Clay changed his name to Cassius X, before finally deciding to go for Muhammad Ali. The decision by Ali became big news at the time and was an issue debated by many. The name change came about when the fighter joined the Nation of Islam, which is a religious organisation.

A new date

A return contest with Sonny Liston was much anticipated by fans of the sport; it was calling out to be made. Many wondered if Ali could win again and retain his world heavyweight crown. Or was it possible that Liston would gain revenge and claim his right to be the top man in the division? The prospect of their second meeting was one that stimulated great interest amongst the public. The wheels were set in motion for the respected bout. However, plans for the said fight were somewhat delayed due to Ali having to undergo surgery on a hernia that needed urgent treatment. This was disappointing to all concerned but a new date for the contest was quickly rescheduled.

Muhammad Ali

On 25 May 1965, Cassius Clay boxed for the first time under the name of Muhammad Ali, knocking out former world champion Sonny Liston in the first round of a proposed fifteen. This was something of a surprise. It always seemed likely that the fight would not go the full distance.

A New Name

Few if any foresaw that it would end this quickly. A real battle had been expected between the two combatants. However, it is always wrong to expect anything in boxing: expectations can be destroyed within a blink of an eye, as this fight fully confirmed. Liston was on a revenge mission and Ali was out to show that he was the better fighter of the two. The ingredients were all there for a dramatic showdown. How could it fail to ignite and produce fireworks?

The defending champion was his usual confident self when entering the ring. He had no doubts that he would depart the ring still wearing the crown. Ali soon showed that his name might now be different but his ring skills were very much the same. He retained the WBC version title of the world heavyweight crown only. The WBA had previously stripped their version of the championship from Ali since he had signed for the return contest with Liston.

A new and exciting era in boxing had now truly begun, with Ali at the helm leading the pack. Ali was now undefeated in twenty-one professional bouts.

The Anchor Punch

To retain his WBC world heavyweight crown by a knockout in the opening round, Muhammad Ali struck Sonny Liston with a blow that was called the 'Phantom Punch'. It was given that name since a number of observers were not convinced that the blow had been that forceful to hurt a man of Liston's hilt or if the punch had even landed at all. However, Ali claimed it was a fight-ending punch, which he had been working on for some time. A blow that he described as the 'Anchor Punch'.

Chapter 8

Stripped of the WBA Title

Jersey Joe Walcott

The referee for the Muhammad Ali and Sonny Liston world title fight was former world heavyweight champion Jersey Joe Walcott, who had reigned from 18 July 1951 to 23 September 1952. This was also the second time that Walcott had been the third man in the ring in a world heavyweight title bout. The first time was the Floyd Patterson title defence against Tom McNeeley on 4 December 1961 at the Maple Leaf Gardens, Toronto, Ontario – a contest that saw the title holder retain his crown by a knockout in round four of a scheduled fifteen.

James J. Jeffries the first

Jersey Joe Walcott was not the first former world heavyweight champion in the history of the sport to referee a world heavyweight title fight. That particular distinction is held by James J. Jeffries, who handled the Marvin Hart–Jack Root contest, which took place at the Amphitheatre, Reno, Nevada on 3 July 1905. Hart won the vacant title (which Jeffries had previously relinquished) when he knocked out Root in round twelve in a fight to the finish. On 28 November 1906, Jeffries once again was the third man in the ring for a world heavyweight title bout when he refereed the Tommy Burns defence of the championship against Philadelphia Jack O' Brien, the venue for the contest being the Naud Junction Pavilion, Los Angeles, California. Burns retained the crown by way of a draw over the duration of twenty rounds. On 4 July 1907, Jeffries stepped into the ring to officiate the Tommy Burns defence against Bill Squires at the Mission Street Arena, Colma, California. The bout was scheduled for forty-five rounds but concluded in the first when Squires was knocked out by the defending champion.

Stripped of the WBA Title

Lowest number of spectators

The return bout between Muhammad Ali and Sonny Liston saw 2,434 spectators witness the championship contest. That reported attendance figure was somewhat disappointing to all concerned since at the time this was the lowest number of spectators ever recorded for a world heavyweight title fight.

Sonny Liston returns to the USA

After his failure to regain his world heavyweight championship from Muhammad Ali, Sonny Liston did not fight again in the USA until 16 March 1968. His return to the States saw him meet Bill McMurray at the Centennial Coliseum, Reno, Nevada. McMurray was no match for Liston and was stopped in the fourth stanza of a ten-round contest. Before this, Liston had participated in four winning bouts in Sweden:

1 July 1966	Gerhard Zech	Won: knockout in round seven of ten
19 August 1966	Amos Johnson	Won: knockout in round three of ten
30 March 1967	Dave Bailey	Won: knockout in round one of ten
28 April 1967	Elmer Rush	Won: stopped in round six of ten

Sonny Liston's last professional contest

After his failure to regain the WBC world heavyweight title from Muhammad Ali, Sonny Liston boxed on and fought another sixteen times, winning fifteen and losing one. The wins being over decent opposition ensured his ranking amongst the top contenders. Even in his later years, Liston was always a threat to the fighters he faced. However, he failed to get another crack at the world crown. Liston had his final bout on 29 June 1970 against opponent Chuck Wepner. Liston bowed out a winner when Wepner retired in round nine of a ten-round contest. The venue for the Liston–Wepner contest was the Armory, Jersey City, New Jersey.

During his career, Sonny Liston participated in fifty-four professional contests, winning fifty and losing four.

Ernie Terrell

On 5 March 1965, Ernie Terrell won the vacant WBA heavyweight crown by outpointing his opponent, Eddie Machen, over the duration of fifteen rounds at the International Amphitheatre, Chicago, Illinois. This situation came about when the WBA stripped their version of the title from Muhammad Ali for going through with his defence against Sonny Liston. Terrell was a good fighter, with a record consisting of forty-fights, winning thirty-six and losing four.

While it goes without saying that it is always fantastic for a boxer to win a world championship, it must be said that under the circumstances it was not really a golden moment for Terrell – far from it. He didn't exactly win the Lottery by winning the championship. In many ways, the title was a curse rather than a blessing. Ali was still recognised by the WBC and the fight fraternity in general as the real world heavyweight king. Terrell was obviously pleased to have the championship status since to some extent it would open the door to bigger and more lucrative fights for him down the line. However, he could not get away from the fact that he was wearing a cardboard crown and would have to eventually meet and defeat Ali to be accepted as the true world heavyweight champion.

Significant impact

On 16 August 1965, a boxer who had won a gold medal at heavyweight at the Tokyo Olympic Games in 1964 made his professional debut at the Convention Hall, Philadelphia, Pennsylvania. Joe Frazier was the fighter in question; he made a great start in the paid ranks by stopping his opponent, Woody Goss, in the opening round of a scheduled six. Frazier looked an exciting addition to the heavyweight division – a boxer who had the potential to go far in the sport. At that moment in time, no one realised that Frazier would reach the very heights of his profession and would have such a significant impact on the career of Muhammad Ali.

Floyd Patterson

After his successful defence over Sonny Liston, Muhammad Ali was raring to go and on 22 November 1965, he made the second defence

Stripped of the WBA Title

of his WBC world heavyweight crown. The fighter in the opposing corner was former two-time title holder Floyd Patterson. The venue for the bout was the Covention Center, Las Vegas. Patterson had won his last five fights since his devastating defeat to Sonny Liston. In his prior contest before meeting Ali, he had a ring outing on 14 May 1965. On that occasion, Patterson met opponent and fellow American Tod Herring at Johanneshov in Stockholm, Sweden. This assignment saw him win in the third round of a scheduled ten. The fight was not a very challenging one for Patterson and there was only ever going to be one winner. The bout only served to give Patterson some ring action before his big moment against Ali. Herring was a decent fighter but Patterson was very much on a different level, and the difference in class was plain to see once they squared off in the ring.

Ali was going to be a much tougher opponent for Patterson than Herring had been. The defending world title holder was a fighter who had achieved his ambition by winning the crown against all the odds. The question now was how long would he be able to hold on to the prized championship? There would be many hungry fighters on his tail, like a pack of angry wolves ready to take the title from him. Patterson in truth did not look like being a serious threat to Ali's reign. So it really wasn't too surprising that Ali was the overwhelming favourite to leave the ring still champion once the fight against his challenger was over.

Ali was at the very peak of his powers, and from here on in was only going to get better in each forthcoming bout. Patterson was a proud fighter who entered the ring believing that he had the experience and the style to upset the odds against him and beat the champion. If he did so, he would become a title holder for a staggering third time. That would be an astonishing achievement. Patterson had to go into the fight with this mindset. He had to have faith in his own ability. While the spectators gave him every support, Patterson fell short in his attempt to take the crown. To his dismay, he found that he did not have the boxing skills to compete on equal terms with the champion. Ali was just too much for him and showed that he was a class above him in every way. This fact became more apparent with the passing of each round. Patterson, like Ali's previous opponents, was at a loss to know what to do against this man. This must have been soul-destroying for him. The challenger was a brave fighter who hung on in the hope that he just might find the punch to turn things in his favour. No one would have blamed Patterson had he bailed out early from the fight, such was the punishment he was taking from Ali. The blood-splatted former two-time world champion was floored in round six. After getting back to his feet he fought on but was always coming off second best in the exchanges, his bruised and swollen features showing the signs of battle. Patterson took his licks and was determined to go out on his shield. His courage could not be faulted; the heart of a champion was still beating strongly in his chest. Eventually, Ali brought the fight to a close when he stopped his challenger in round twelve of a scheduled fifteen.

Throughout the bout, Ali fought without extending himself against Patterson, giving a display that was punch perfect. Ali had now boosted his perfect record to an undefeated twenty-two bouts. While Patterson's resume now boasted a slate of forty-eight fights, winning forty-three and losing five.

First man to have regained the world heavyweight championship

Floyd Patterson at the time of his challenge to Muhammad Ali was the only boxer to have regained the world heavyweight championship in the long history of the sport. Patterson had first lost the crown on 26 June 1959 at the Yankee Stadium, Bronx, New York, when stopped in round three of fifteen by Sweden's Ingemar Johansson. This was a massive upset and was the first time that a non-American had held the title since Italy's Primo Carnera, who reigned from 1933 to 1934. Patterson was desperate to put matters right and return the title back to the USA.

A chance for redemption for Patterson took place on 20 June 1960 at the Polo Grounds, New York. He gained sweet revenge when he knocked out Johansson in round five of a scheduled fifteen to become king of the division once again, thus ensuring his place in the history of the sport. Patterson was later shorn of his crown by Sonny Liston, on 25 September 1962 at Comiskey Park, Chicago, when he was knocked out in the opening round in a contest scheduled for fifteen. Patterson then stepped back into the ring at the Convention Center, Las Vegas, with Liston on 22 July 1963, hoping to redeem himself by regaining the title for a second time. This was not going to happen. Liston was far more dangerous than Johansson and was not likely to wilt under the fists of Patterson. The fight proved to be more than just a nightmare for the former champion since once again he was destroyed by the hard-punching Liston in the first stanza in a fight that was never going to go the full distance of fifteen rounds.

Patterson challenged Ellis

Floyd Patterson had one more attempt to regain a version of the world heavyweight championship on 14 September 1968. He travelled to Sweden to challenge the then WBA title holder Jimmy Ellis. It seemed that Patterson would have a better chance of beating Ellis than he had of beating Muhammad Ali. A win here by Patterson would have seen him become the first man to regain the crown twice. This would have been something special. However, it was not to be. The venue for the contest was the Råsunda Fotbollsstadion, Stockholm. The bout went the full distance of fifteen rounds, whereby Ellis turned back Patterson by retaining the crown with a points decision. Patterson had now competed in thirteen world heavyweight title bouts.

Chapter 9

Ali Meets Cooper for a Second Time

Full championship distance

On 29 March 1966, Muhammad Ali travelled across the border to Canada, where, at the Maple Leaf Gardens, Toronto, he made the third defence of his WBC world heavyweight crown. The challenger in the opposite corner was the experienced Canadian, George Chuvalo, who came with a slate of forty-seven bouts, winning thirty-four, losing eleven and drawing two.

The Canadian was coming into the bout after losing his previous contest on 25 January 1966 to Argentine-born Eduardo Corletti by way of a ten-round points decision at the Olympia in Kensington, London. This did not inspire a great deal of confidence for the challenger's chances against Ali. Corletti was a good fighter but he was nowhere near Ali's class. This was Chuvalo's second attempt to win the title at heavyweight. The Canadian had previously challenged Ernie Terrell for the WBA version on 1 November 1965. The venue for the bout had also been the Maple Leaf Gardens. Chuvalo was not able to get the better of the champion during the battle and failed in his bid. Terrell retained the crown with a fifteen-round points decision.

Ali entered the ring undefeated in twenty-two contests. Chuvalo had been in the game for some years and was not in awe of the man he was about to face. As expected, the Canadian showed no hesitancy against Ali and attacked constantly, proving to be a tough competitor with an iron will to go with his granite chin. Chuvalo never gave up during the contest, with his never-say-die attitude looking for the opening to land his punches. For the first time in his career, Ali had to go the full championship distance of fifteen rounds to retain his title with a points decision. Once again, in his bout with Chuvalo, Ali revealed that he was the master of the ring and it would take someone very special to take the championship from him. Looking at the list of contenders in the weight category at the time, it appeared that Ali was set to reign for some considerable time.

You needed punching power

It was unlikely that Muhammad Ali would stop George Chuvalo when defending his WBC world heavyweight title bout. While Ali was a most skilful boxer, he was not renowned for being a big puncher, and you needed serious punching power if you were to halt Chuvalo. The only time the Canadian failed to go the distance in a contest was on 2 October 1961, when he lost by a disqualification in round five of ten. That defeat came in Toronto against Welshman Joe Erskine, the former British and Commonwealth heavyweight champion.

First time in Canada

The Muhammad Ali–George Chuvalo bout was the third time that a world heavyweight title fight had been staged in Canada. The first was the Floyd Patterson defence against Tom McNeeley, which had taken place on 4 December 1961. McNeeley was not from Canada, he was from the USA, so there was no real interest for Canadian fans except for the fact that a world heavyweight title bout was being staged in their country. The venue for the Patterson–McNeeley contest was the Maple Leaf Gardens in Toronto. Patterson retained his championship when he knocked out his challenger in round four of fifteen

Last world heavyweight champion from Canada

The fans in attendance at the Muhammad Ali–George Chuvalo contest were clearly hoping for a victory for the home fighter, which was only natural. They badly wanted their man to win and return the crown to Canada. It was, in reality, a forlorn hope, for Ali was at the very peak of his powers. He looked unbeatable and he relished the prospect of meeting his latest challenger. There were no chinks in the champion's armour; if there were any, Chuvalo was unable to find them. The title holder looked supreme in the division at this stage in his career – a very special fighter who appeared set to take boxing to another level. At the time, Canada's last world champion in the division was Tommy Burns, who had reigned from 1906 to 1908.

A short record

Tommy Burns is the holder of a very unique record in boxing – not one where he had won more fights inside the distance than any other participant, or indeed one where he had made more title defences than any other champion at the weight. Burns, in fact, holds the record of being the shortest man to win the world heavyweight title. His recorded height was 5 feet 7 inches, which seems incredible. This is a record that the Canadian will surely keep, especially when considering how tall modern-day fighters are in the division. Burns won the crown on 23 February 1906 when outpointing American holder Marvin Hart over twenty rounds at the Pacific Athletic Club in Los Angeles. He eventually lost his crown to Jack Johnson on 26 December 1908 at the Sydney Stadium, New South Wales, Australia. The bout was halted in round fourteen in Johnson's favour.

George Chuvalo's last professional contest

After failing to take the world heavyweight crown from Muhammad Ali, George Chuvalo continued with his boxing career, participating in forty-five more fights, winning thirty-nine and losing six. He engaged in his last contest on 11 December 1978, which proved to be a winning one for him when making a successful defence of his Canadian heavyweight title. He stopped his challenger, George Jerome, in round three of a scheduled twelve. The venue for the Chuvalo–Jerome fight was St Lawrence Market in Toronto.

George Chuvalo participated in ninety-three professional fights during his career, winning seventy-three, losing eighteen and drawing two.

Ali Meets Cooper for a Second Time

Back to the UK

It was a return trip to the UK for Muhammad Ali on 21 May 1966 when he put his WBC world heavyweight title on the line against challenger and former opponent Henry Cooper. On this occasion Ali became the first fighter from the USA to defend the heavyweight title in the UK. The venue for the contest was the Arsenal Football Stadium, Highbury, London. This was obviously big news and an occasion to look forward to, with much speculation about Cooper's chances of victory.

Ali was now recognised worldwide as not just a champion, but a special champion, who was a brilliant ring technician. He was a fighter who was bringing something fresh to the sport of boxing, adding a new dimension to the game. Ali had a sharp brain and was able to negate the dangers his opponents presented. It was obvious that he was more than aware of the British fighter's potent left hook, having felt its power in their first meeting, which had taken place on 18 June 1963 at Wembley Stadium and had seen him put on the canvas. It was a night he was not likely to forget in a hurry. It was a case of once bitten, twice shy. Ali had no intention of getting caught again by the British fighter's potentially fight-ending punch. It is often said that lightening doesn't strike twice in the same place. Ali was determined that Cooper's left hook would not strike twice. He came into the ring with an undefeated record of twenty-three bouts. Cooper climbed through the ropes with a resume of forty-five fights, which consisted of thirty-three wins, eleven defeats and one draw.

Since their last bout, Cooper had fought on eight occasions, winning six and losing two. Prior to this meeting with Ali for the world crown, he had despatched Jefferson Davis, who was from the USA, by way of a knockout in the first round of a scheduled ten. The bout had taken place on 16 February 1966 at the Civic Hall, Wolverhampton, in the West Midlands. It was a good victory by Cooper, who looked impressive, but truth be told, Jefferson was nowhere near the standard of Ali. The big question now was could Cooper succeed where Sonny Liston, Floyd Patterson and George Chuvalo had failed? The opinion of many prior to the fight was a very definite no. It was felt that Ali would return to the USA still champion of the world.

The nation was fully behind Cooper and cheered his every move as the fight got underway. The challenger forced the fight from the first stanza, attempting to land his left hook on Ali in his brave bid to add the crown to his name. Cooper's attempt to win the title was foiled when he was stopped in round six of fifteen due to a cut over his left eye. The cut was bad; the blood ran freely from his wound in a crimson river down his cheek. Once the damage became obvious, the fans knew that the fight was over. You did not need any medical training to know that the Briton could not go on. This was the end of the line for Cooper. Had there been an award in boxing for the worst cut in a world title fight that year, Cooper's name would have been at the top of the list of candidates. He had tried his best but was being conquered by the fast-punching champion who was moving gracefully around the ring with the speed of a middleweight. It was a good result for the defending champion but a depressing one for fans of UK boxing, who badly wanted to see a Briton wear the crown. Every time a British contender challenged for the world heavyweight title, they came off second best.

While Ali was around and on top of the tree, there seemed little hope that the situation would change. The man looked like being a king for a long time, such was his dominance in the division.

A record for British boxing

The Muhammad Ali–Henry Cooper WBC world heavyweight title fight sparked a great deal of interest in Britain. So much so that the contest drew a reported 46,000 spectators, which was a staggering number. That figure created a record for British boxing at the time since it was the largest audience for a boxing show in the UK.

First British promoter

Harry Levene was the promoter of the WBC world heavyweight title bout between Muhammad Ali and Henry Cooper. In so doing, he became the first British promoter to stage a world championship fight in Europe involving Muhammad Ali.

Levene had been involved in many top promotions during his career; he drew great acclaim at the time by bringing the best of the best together inside the ring. However, the Ali–Cooper contest must rate as one of his greatest promotional triumphs in boxing.

Bob Fitzsimmons

By the time of Henry Cooper's challenge to Muhammad Ali, the UK had waited long for a world champion in the division. Britain's first world heavyweight champion had been Bob Fitzsimmons, who won the title on 17 March 1897. Cornwall-born Fitzsimmons had claimed the crown when he knocked out the defending title holder James J. Corbett in round fourteen in a fight to the finish. The contest between Fitzsimmons and Corbett took place at the Race Track Arena, Carson City, Nevada. Fitzsimmons later lost the championship in his first defence to James J. Jeffries on 9 June 1899, when knocked out in the eleventh stanza in a bout that was scheduled for twenty. The contest was staged at Coney Island Athletic Club, Brooklyn, New York.

First Scot

George Smith of Edinburgh was the third man in the ring during the Muhammad Ali–Henry Cooper bout and hence made history by becoming the first official from Scotland to referee a world heavyweight title bout.

Chapter 10

London Challenges Ali

Sir Henry Cooper

Henry Cooper did not get a second shot at the world heavyweight title after his defeat to Muhammad Ali. The British fighter did however continue his career with a good degree of success without the aid of holding a world crown in the division. Cooper made boxing history by being the first boxer to be knighted – a remarkable honour indeed for him and for the sport of boxing.

Ali defeated a future Knight of the Realm

Muhammad Ali can proudly lay claim to many honours earned during his distinguished career in the ring. There is yet another, somewhat unusual, one that he can add to the list. He became the first world heavyweight champion from the USA to have defeated a future Knight of the Realm. He did so when defeating Henry Cooper in defence of his WBC world heavyweight title on 21 May 1966.

First to win three Lonsdale Belts outright

Henry Cooper may have failed to win the WBC world heavyweight title belt from Muhammad Ali, but it would be true to say that he was not short of championship belts on the domestic front. Cooper made history when he became the first to win three Lonsdale belts outright for defences of the British heavyweight crown. When Cooper was fighting, a boxer had to win three title contests to win a belt outright.

London Challenges Ali

Cooper thus won nine title bouts to obtain the belts. He even put the first notch on a fourth belt. Due to a later rule change, a boxer can now win only one belt outright in any one division and needs to win four championship bouts to do so. Clearly, no one will ever equal Cooper's record in the future, or indeed surpass it. All bouts were set for the duration of fifteen rounds.

The list below details the opponents Cooper defeated to win the respected belts and the venues where the fights took place:

Brian London won title on points over fifteen rounds   12 January 1959
    (Venue: Earls Court Arena, Kensington, London)
Joe Erskine won by twelfth-round stoppage   17 November 1959
    (Venue: Earls Court Arena, Kensington, London)
Joe Erskine won, stopped in round five   21 March 1961
    (Venue: Empire Pool, Wembley, London)
Joe Erskine won by ninth-round stoppage)   2 April 1962
    (Venue: Ice Rink, Nottingham)
Dick Richardson won by knockout, round five   26 March 1963
    (Venue: Empire Pool, Wembley, London)
Brian London won on points over fifteen rounds*   24 February 1964
    (Venue: Kings Hall, Belle Vue, Manchester)
Johnny Prescott won, retired in round ten   15 June 1965
    (Venue: St Andrews (Birmingham City FC), Birmingham)
Jack Bodell won by stoppage in round two   13 June 1967
    (Venue: Molineux Grounds, Wolverhampton)
Billy Walker won by stoppage in round six   17 November 1967
    (Venue: Empire Pool, Wembley, London)
Jack Bodell won on points over fifteen rounds and regained British title after previously relinquishing it   24 March 1970
    (Venue: Empire Pool, Wembley, London)
Joe Bugner lost title over fifteen rounds*   16 March 1971
(Venue: Empire Pool, Wembley, London)

Note: all bouts also involved the Commonwealth title and * included the European crown.

Almost a second shot

Henry Cooper almost secured a second shot at the world heavyweight championship in 1969. This chance came about when Jimmy Ellis, the then reigning WBA title holder, agreed to meet Cooper in defence of his title. However, the British Boxing Board of Control refused to sanction the fight because they were not affiliated to the WBA. Cooper in response relinquished his British heavyweight crown in protest at the decision made by the Board. Despite this, plans to stage the fight went ahead anyway. It seemed fate was very much against Cooper since he had to have surgery on his knee, which made him unable to fight Ellis. Sadly, some things in life are just not meant to be.

Henry Cooper's last professional contest

After his failed WBC world heavyweight title challenge to Muhammad Ali, Henry Cooper fought on and took part in another nine bouts, of which he won seven and lost two. Cooper made his last ring appearance on 16 March 1971, losing his British, European and Commonwealth heavyweight crowns to Joe Bugner by way of a fifteen-round points decision. The venue for the Cooper–Bugner contest was the Empire Pool, Wembley. Cooper in his time was a hero to British fight fans and a great ambassador for the sport.

During his professional career, Henry Cooper participated in fifty-five bouts, winning forty, losing fourteen and drawing one.

First world heavyweight title bout since 1950

The Muhammad Ali–Henry Cooper bout was the first world heavyweight title contest to be staged in the UK since 6 June 1950. On that occasion, it once again proved to be a disappointment for British fans since American Lee Savold won the vacant BBB of C version of the championship when he defeated Bruce Woodcock, who retired in round four of a slated fifteen due to a bad cut over his left eyebrow. Prior to the bout, it looked as if Woodcock would have a good chance of victory over his opponent from the USA and have his name added to the list of world title holders. Woodcock had previously defeated Savold on 6 December 1948 by a disqualification in round four of ten in a bout that took place at the Harringay Arena, London. It was hoped he could repeat the win, but it wasn't to be. The venue for the Savold–Woodcock bout was the White City Stadium, London. The title that Savold won did not hold a great deal of credence at the time.

On the other side of the Atlantic, Ezzard Charles was the holder of the NBA heavyweight version of the title, which he had won on 22 June 1949 by defeating Jersey Joe Walcott on points over fifteen rounds. The Charles–Walcott contest had taken place at Comiskey Park, Chicago, Illinois. This fight was made following the retirement of Joe Louis. Many regarded Charles's claim to the championship to be much stronger than Savold's.

London's world title bid against Ali

In a third visit to the UK, Muhammad Ali successfully defended his WBC world heavyweight title for the fifth time. The venue was the Earls Court Arena, Kensington, London. Ali knocked out challenger Brian London, the former British and Commonwealth title holder, in the third round of fifteen on 6 August 1966. Ali entered the ring against London with an undefeated record of twenty-four fights.

The home challenger brought a resume of forty-eight bouts, with thirty-five wins and thirteen defeats, so he was not exactly wet behind the ears when it came to boxing. He had been involved in the sport for a number of years. London had made a promising start to his professional debut on 22 March 1955, stopping his opponent Dennis Lockton in the first round of six at the Earls Court Empress Hall, Kensington. Before entering the ring with Ali to challenge for the title, London had suffered a previous defeat on 2 May 1966 at the King's Hall, Belle Vue, Manchester, against Thad Spencer from the USA. The American left the ring with a victory under his belt when he outpointed him over ten rounds. At that time, London appeared to have very little chance of ever sharing the ring with Ali for the world heavyweight title. However, there is a very old saying, 'Never say die', and that often applies in boxing. London put that defeat against Spencer behind him and was soon back in action, and on 21 June 1966, he secured a victory at The Stadium, Liverpool, where he defeated Amos Johnson, who hailed from the USA, by way of a disqualification in round seven of a scheduled ten. This was not an earth-shattering result – not one that made pundits sit up and think that this man just might give Ali problems.

Whilst it may have been the wish of many British fans, London was not expected to be the fighter to end the long wait the UK had endured for a world heavyweight king. If there was a blueprint for defeating Ali, London clearly did not have it in his possession. From the first round, it was painfully obvious that London would not be able to cope with the champion. Ali was too quick for him. At no time did the American look threatened, nor was he under any kind of pressure from his challenger. The Briton was truly outclassed over the duration of the contest. London's challenge was disappointingly short lived. However, London did acquire at the time the distinction of being the first British fighter in modern times to challenge twice for the heavyweight crown.

Brian London's first bid for the heavyweight crown

Brian London's first attempt to win a world heavyweight title had taken place on 1 May 1959 at the Fairgrounds Coliseum, Indianapolis, Indiana, USA. His challenge came against the then undisputed champion, Floyd Patterson. In this bid, London lasted longer than he did against Muhammad Ali but the outcome was the same. The American dispatched London in round eleven of a scheduled fifteen by way of a knockout.

Second time for Solomons

The promoters of the Muhammad Ali–Brian London WBC world heavyweight title bout were Jack Solomons and Lawrie Lewis. This was the second time that Solomons had been involved in an Ali promotion. He had previously brought Muhammad Ali (then Cassius Clay) to England to fight Henry Cooper. The respected contest took place on

18 June 1963, whereupon Cooper was stopped in the fifth round of ten. The venue for the bout was Wembley Stadium, London. In 1978, Solomons was awarded an OBE for his charitable services.

Harry Gibbs

Harry Gibbs was the third man in charge of the Muhammad Ali–Brian London world heavyweight title fight. Gibbs, a well-respected official, became the second British referee to handle a world title bout that involved Ali.

Chapter 11

Ali Defends Against Mildenberger

Brian London's last professional contest

After his failed world heavyweight title bid to Muhammad Ali, Brian London fought on and had a further nine bouts, winning two and losing six, with one drawn. The curtain finally came down on London's career on 12 May 1970 at the Empire Pool, Wembley. The former British and Commonwealth heavyweight champion decided to hang up his gloves and quit the ring when he was stopped in the fifth of a ten-round contest by Joe Bugner. The decision to retire was the right course of action. The writing was on the wall as far as the fighter's career was concerned. London was clearly past his best and really had nowhere to go after his defeat to Bugner.

During his professional career, Brian London participated in fifty-eight bouts, winning thirty-seven, losing twenty, and drawing one.

Successive world title defence against British challengers

In defeating Brian London, on 6 August 1966 Muhammad Ali became the first world heavyweight champion from the USA to defend his title against two British challengers in succession. Prior to Brian London, Ali had defeated Henry Cooper on 21 May 1966 at the Arsenal Football Stadium, Highbury, London, by a stoppage in round six of fifteen.

First southpaw challenger

Muhammad Ali became the first world heavyweight champion in the history of the sport to defend his title against a challenger with the southpaw stance. This event took place on 10 September 1966.

Ali Defends Against Mildenberger

The venue for the contest was the Waldstadion/Radrennbahn, Frankfurt, Germany. The challenger was Karl Mildenberger, the reigning European title holder, who had a professional record of fifty-four bouts, winning forty-nine, losing two, with three drawn. Mildenberger was a good exponent of the sweet science but he, like so many before him, was no match for the American. Mildenberger had his moments in the bout but they were few and far between. The gulf in class between Ali and the other fighters in the weight division was extremely wide at this time. Ali thus made a sixth successful defence of the championship by way of a stoppage in round twelve in a bout scheduled for fifteen. Ali was now undefeated in twenty-six contests.

First in Germany

The Muhammad Ali–Karl Mildenberger contest secured its place in the boxing history books by becoming the first world heavyweight championship bout to be staged in Germany.

Karl Mildenberger's last professional contest

After being defeated by Muhammad Ali when challenging for the WBC world heavyweight title, Karl Mildenberger's career continued with mixed success. He took part in another seven bouts, winning four and losing three. Mildenberger had his last contest on 18 September 1968, losing his European heavyweight crown to Henry Cooper at the Empire Pool, Wembley, by a disqualification in round eight of a scheduled fifteen.

During his professional career Karl Mildenberger participated in sixty-two bouts, winning fifty-three, losing six and drawing three

Max Schmeling

Karl Mildenberger fought bravely against Muhammad Ali in his bid for the world heavyweight championship, giving the title holder a more difficult time than expected. Mildenberger was no mug; he brought into the ring everything he had learnt about boxing over the years, and that was considerable. However, Mildenberger's skills and experience meant very little on the night against the defending champion. Ali was clearly on a higher level than his challenger, and was in control throughout the fight. Had Mildenberger been successful in his attempt to win the crown he would have been Germany's first holder of the title since Max Schmeling, who reigned from 1930 to 1932.

Schmeling holds the record

Max Schmeling holds the record for being the first man to win the world heavyweight title by way of a four-round disqualification. The contest in question was against Jack Sharkey in a bout that was set for the duration of fifteen rounds and took place on 12 June 1930. The bout was for the vacant crown after Gene Tunney had relinquished the title. The Schmeling–Sharkey contest took place at the Yankee Stadium, Bronx, New York. Sharkey was disqualified by the referee when he incapacitated Schmeling by hitting him with a low blow.

Teddy Waltham

The third man in the ring for the Muhammad Ali–Karl Mildenberger WBC world heavyweight title contest was the UK's Teddy Waltham, an experienced referee who had over the years been in charge of a number of bouts that involved British, Commonwealth, European and world championships in various weight divisions. However, the Ali–Mildenberger bout was the first time that he had refereed a world heavyweight championship fight.

Three in succession

When Teddy Waltham was appointed as the referee for the Muhammad Ali–Karl Mildenberger WBC world heavyweight title fight it was a special occasion for the UK. For the first time in the history of the sport, British boxing officials had refereed three successive world heavyweight title bouts, all of which had involved Ali. The previous two UK referees were:

George Smith   Ali v Cooper, 21 May 1966 at the Arsenal Football Stadium, Highbury, London.
Harry Gibbs   Ali v London, 6 August 1966 at Earls Court Arena, Kensington, London.

Have gloves, will travel

When defending his crown against Karl Mildenberger, Muhammad Ali became the first world heavyweight champion from the USA to make four successive defences of his title outside of the USA. The said countries were: Canada, England (twice) and Germany. Ali's suitcase and passport was clearly in constant use during this period. It was a case of 'have gloves will travel' for the reigning world title holder.

Two of Muhammad Ali's former challengers

Floyd Patterson and Henry Cooper returned to the ring on 20 September 1966. Both boxers had lost in their previous contest when bidding for the WBC world heavyweight title against defending champion Muhammad Ali. The Patterson and Cooper bout took place at the Empire Pool, Wembley, in a contest scheduled for ten rounds. There was a great deal riding on this bout for both fighters since the winner could once again figure in a future world title fight. The home fans were hoping that Cooper would come out on top and they gave him every encouragement during the action. It was Patterson who emerged victorious when he knocked out Cooper in the fourth round. This was the first time that two of Ali's challengers had fought each other after losing to him in their previous bouts.

Chapter 12

Undisputed World Champion

A magnificent display

Muhammad Ali successfully retained his WBC world heavyweight crown on 14 November 1966 for the seventh time. He did so when he made short work of his challenger, Cleveland Williams, by dispassionately stopping him in round three of fifteen at the Astrodome, Houston, Texas. Williams came into the battle with a resume of seventy-six bouts, winning sixty-nine and losing five, with two drawn. That was some record – one to respect and one be a little fearful of.

In his last outing before facing Ali, Williams had easily stopped Tod Herring in round three of ten at the Sam Houston Coliseum, Houston, on 28 June 1966. Williams had last experienced defeat at the hands of Ernie Terrell on 13 April 1963 by a ten-round points decision at the Philadelphia Arena, Pennsylvania. Since that setback, Williams had regrouped and won his last nine bouts in a row so he was primed and ready for his crack at the championship. Williams was a true warrior and a noted puncher who had the explosive power to end a contest quickly should his glove find its target. Yet the power means nothing if you cannot land the damaging blow on your opponent. Ali was never going to be a stationary opponent. He was too quick and too sharp for his challenger. Ali had the speed of foot to be able to avoid with ease the missiles that came his way.

The fight was an exciting one while it lasted and a number of observers at the time felt that this was Ali at his very best, giving a magnificent display of boxing against a very dangerous challenger. The champion was on fire from the first bell, and Williams felt the heat and got badly burnt in the process. Williams was nicknamed 'The Cat' but it was Ali who was purring with success at the bout's conclusion. Ali was now undefeated in twenty-seven professional outings.

Record number of spectators

The Muhammad Ali–Cleveland Williams WBC world heavyweight title contest created a great deal of interest amongst the public. It was clearly a fight many fans wanted to see. The popularity of the bout resulted in the fight creating a record by registering the largest number of spectators to witness an indoor boxing contest to date. The total was a reported 35,460.

The Ali shuffle

During the world heavyweight title defence against Cleveland Williams, the confident Muhammad Ali displayed the fancy footwork called the 'Ali shuffle', much to the pleasure of those in attendance. This was a move that dancing legend Fred Astaire might very well have been impressed with.

Muhammad Ali back on USA soil

The WBC World heavyweight title defence against Cleveland Williams was the first time that the globetrotting Muhammad Ali had fought in the USA since his successful defence against Floyd Patterson. The Clay–Patterson contest had taken place on 22 November 1965 – a bout that saw Ali retain his world crown by stopping Patterson in round twelve of a scheduled fifteen. The title fight had taken place at the Convention Center, Las Vegas, Nevada.

Cleveland Williams's last professional contest

After being defeated by Muhammad Ali in his world heavyweight title challenge, Cleveland Williams fought on and took part in a further twenty fights, winning thirteen and losing seven. Williams had been a popular fighter, one who never backed away from meeting the best in the division and one who was exciting to watch when in action, win or lose. His last contest took place on 28 October 1972, whereupon he left the sport on a winning note after he outpointed opponent Roberto Davila over ten rounds at the Denver Coliseum, Colorado.

During his career, Cleveland Williams participated in ninety-seven professional bouts, of which he won eighty-two, lost thirteen and drew two.

Five defences

The year 1966 was a very busy one for Muhammad Ali, since the champion made five successful defences of the WBC world heavyweight title. This was good for the sport since Ali was not keeping the crown in cold storage. The title holder was putting the championship on the line at every available opportunity. This was the most Ali would ever defend the championship in one calendar year during his career.

Joe Louis's seven defences

The five defences made by Muhammad Ali were indeed impressive. However, it should be noted that he was not able to surpass the record of successful defences in one calendar year made by Joe Louis. Louis was very active in 1941, making seven defences against the following challengers at the stated venues:

Red Burman, knocked out in round five of fifteen (Venue: Madison Square Garden, New York)	31 January
Gus Dorazio, knocked out in round two of fifteen (Venue: Convention Hall, Philadelphia, Pennsylvania)	17 February
Abe Simon, stopped in round thirteen of twenty (Venue: Olympia Stadium, Detroit, Michigan)	21 March
Tony Musto, stopped in round nine of fifteen (Venue: Arena, Saint Louis, Missouri)	8 April
Buddy Baer, disqualified in round seven of fifteen (Venue: Griffith Stadium, Washington District of Columbia)	23 May
Billy Conn, knocked out in round thirteen of fifteen (Venue: Polo Grounds, New York)	18 June
Lou Nova, stopped in round six of fifteen (Venue: Polo Grounds, New York)	29 September

Unified title

At the Houston Astrodome in Texas, Muhammad Ali (WBC) and Ernie Terrell (WBA) met in a unification contest on 6 February 1967. Terrell had won the vacant WBA crown on 5 March 1965 when he outpointed Eddie Machen over fifteen rounds at the International Amphitheatre, Chicago, Illinois. The WBA had stripped their version of the title from Ali when he met Sonny Liston in a return contest.

It would be true to say that despite Terrell's claim to a version of the championship, Ali was still regarded as the true title holder in the division – there was no getting away from that one vital fact. The bout against Ali was Terrell's third defence of the title he was holding. He had previously turned back the challenge of George Chuvalo on 1 November 1965, at the Maple Leaf Gardens, Toronto, Ontario, by way of a fifteen-round points decision. Then, Doug Jones challenged Terrell on 28 June 1966 at the Sam Houston Coliseum, Houston, Texas. The champion kept his crown with a fifteen-round points victory.

In the course of his career, Terrell had comprised a record of forty-three fights, with thirty-nine victories and four defeats, before his meeting with Ali. That was a good resume, one that suggested he would make a real fight of it against Ali in his attempt to unify the title. It was not a good night for Terrell. Most of us get the occasional nightmare when we are asleep in bed. Terrell had his nightmare when he was very much awake, in the ring, with Ali. It was a nightmare he would not forget in hurry. Any hopes Terrell had of defeating Ali soon disappeared with the passing of each round. The fight proved to be a very painful encounter for the WBA title holder. Terrell may have lasted the full fifteen rounds with Ali but he took a systematic beating and was clearly outpointed. He bravely remained on his feet throughout the bout, not taking a count at any time from the referee. While he had the satisfaction of going the distance with Ali, the price of doing so was costly since he was badly battered at the end of the contest. Ali left the ring still undefeated in twenty-eight bouts and was now the undisputed title holder at the weight.

What's my name?

There was a great deal of animosity between Muhammad Ali and Ernie Terrell due to the fact that Terrell refused to call Ali by his name, constantly referring to him as Cassius Clay. This greatly annoyed Ali since he regarded Clay as his slave name. Ali's anger boiled over in a bad-tempered press conference and also throughout the duration of the title fight. During the course of the unification contest, Ali would often taunt Terrell by saying, 'What's My Name?'

The tallest man

When looking at the big picture it may be true to say that this fact is not much consolation for the defeat against Muhammad Ali. However, Ernie Terrell can lay claim to being the tallest man to have boxed Ali in a world heavyweight title contest, at the reported height of 6 feet 6 inches.

Harry Kessler

The experienced Harry Kessler refereed both the Muhammad Ali–Cleveland Williams and Muhammad Ali–Ernie Terrell world heavyweight title bouts during his career. In so doing, he became the first and only official to referee two Muhammad Ali world title fights in succession.

Chapter 13

Frazier and Ellis become Champions

Ernie Terrell's last professional contest

Ernie Terrell continued his career after losing to Muhammad Ali in their unified world heavyweight title contest. Terrell took part in a further eleven bouts, of which he won seven and lost four. His farewell to boxing took place on 10 September 1973, when he was stopped in the opening stanza by Jeff Merritt – a defeat that made it obvious that his time in the ring was over and this was the right moment to say goodbye to the sport. The Terrell–Merritt fight took place at Madison Square Garden, New York. The bout was scheduled for ten rounds.

During his professional career, Ernie Terrell participated in fifty-five bouts, winning forty-six and losing nine.

Ali's last professional bout before exile

Ali was back in the saddle once more and ready to do business – ready once again to display his skills and prove that he was without question the best heavyweight boxer in the world. At Madison Square Garden, New York, he retained his undisputed world heavyweight crown against the ringwise challenger Zora Folley. The win came by way of a knockout in round seven of fifteen. Folley was an experienced and respected campaigner who had been around the sport for a long time and had met a number of top fighters during his career. He entered the ring with a record of eighty-five bouts, winning seventy-four and losing seven, with four drawn. Folley had last seen action on 17 January 1967, when he made short work of opponent Floyd Joyner, knocking him out in the first of a bout scheduled for ten rounds. The contest had taken place at the Coliseum, Houston, Texas. His last defeat came on 27 July 1963 at the hands of Ernie Terrell, when he was outpointed over ten rounds at Madison Square Garden. Since that setback, Folley had fought on twelve occasions, winning eleven, with one drawn. The ten-round draw came against Karl Mildenberger on 17 April 1964 at the Festhalle, Frankfurt, Germany.

The champion entered the combat zone against Folley with the perfect resume of twenty-eight bouts without tasting defeat. The contest between Ali and Folley took place on 22 March 1967. While Folley was a proven world-class fighter, no one truthfully felt that the title would change hands on the night. Folley had waited a long time for a shot at the title, maybe too long. Now that his chance had finally come for a crack at the title, he was facing an outstanding champion, a man who was very much in his prime – a fighter who was unbeatable, a man who would most certainly maintain that status when the fight with Folley was over. The challenger presented very little danger to the defending champion. That may sound harsh but it was true. Ali controlled the fight from the first bell and looked comfortable at all times during the contest. He used his fast left jab to good effect, picking off his man easily. This proved to be Ali's last defence of the crown before being stripped of the title due to his refusal to be inducted into the US Army.

Zora Folley's last professional contest

After his failure to capture the world heavyweight crown from Muhammad Ali, Zora Folley continued his ring career. He fought a further ten times, winning five, losing three and drawing two of his contests. Folley had his last outing at the Selland Arena, Fresno, California, on 29 September 1970, where he was knocked out in round one in a contest scheduled for the duration of ten by opponent Mac Foster. It was a sensible move for Folley to now bid farewell to the sport rather than to go on and become a stepping-stone for up-and-coming fighters who wanted a good name on their resume.

During his professional career, Zora Folley had participated in ninety-six bouts, winning seventy-nine, losing eleven and drawing six.

Frazier and Ellis become Champions

Frazier claims version of the world heavyweight title

The vacant NYSAC world heavyweight crown was at stake on 4 March 1968 at Madison Square Garden, New York, when Joe Frazier stepped into the ring to meet Buster Mathis. Both fighters were undefeated in the professional ranks – Frazier in nineteen bouts and Mathis in twenty-three. The match had all the requirements to be a crowd-pleasing slugfest. Frazier was the favourite going into the bout and confirmed why when he won the title in style by stopping Mathis in round eleven of fifteen. Mathis gave it his all and was not fearful of the puncher who shared the ring with him. He was determined to defeat Frazier and take the crown. While the title on the line was only a fractured version of the championship, it still had value; it was a title that would open doors, giving the victor recognition.

Frazier proved too powerful for his opponent. Mathis was soundly outboxed and outpunched. There was now a new champion in town – even if only a part champion who looked to have the skill set to light up the division. The vacant title that Frazier and Mathis fought for came about when Muhammad Ali was stripped of his championship.

Third Olympic gold medallist to win a version of the world heavyweight title

When Joe Frazier captured the vacant NYSAC world heavyweight championship by defeating Buster Mathis, he became the third former Olympic gold medallist to hold a version of the title, the other two being Floyd Patterson (middleweight) and Muhammad Ali (light-heavyweight).

Jimmy Ellis wins WBA world heavyweight title

On 27 April 1968, Jimmy Ellis won the vacant WBA version of the world heavyweight title when he outpointed opponent Jerry Quarry at the Coliseum Arena, Oakland, California. Ellis took the crown on points when he outpointed Quarry over the duration of fifteen rounds. Going into the bout Ellis had a record of thirty fights, with twenty-five wins and five defeats. Quarry had a slate of thirty-one bouts, with twenty-six wins and one defeat, with four drawn. Prior to the fight, it was not easy to predict with confidence who the eventual winner would be. This was the final of a tournament held by the WBA to find a successor to Muhammad Ali, who had been stripped of the crown. If anything, the fight between Ellis and Quarry had clearly outlined the void created in the division by the absence of Ali. Top-rated fighters like Floyd Patterson, Karl Mildenberger, Leotis Martin, Oscar Bonavena, Ernie Terrell and Thad Spencer had also competed in the tournament but were eliminated along the way to the final, leaving Ellis and Quarry to duke it out for the title.

Third world heavyweight champion from Louisville

When Jimmy Ellis won the WBA world heavyweight crown, he became the third from Louisville, Kentucky, to do so. The first was Marvin Hart, who captured the vacant title on 3 July 1905 when he knocked out opponent Jack Root in round twelve in a fight to the finish. The bout took place at the Amphitheatre, Reno, Nevada.

The second world heavyweight champion from Louisville was, of course, Muhammad Ali, who famously won the crown from Sonny Liston, who retired in his corner in round six on 25 February 1964 at the Convention Center, Miami Beach, Florida.

The large shadow of Muhammad Ali

On 16 February 1970, Joe Frazier and Jimmy Ellis met at Madison Square Garden, New York, in a unification heavyweight world title fight to find the undisputed champion in the absence of Muhammad Ali. Frazier held the NYSAC version of the championship and was making his fifth defence of the crown. Ellis wore the WBA crown and this was his second defence of the title. The vacant WBC title was also on the line in this bout. Frazier was undefeated in twenty-four bouts while Ellis had amassed a total of thirty-two fights, winning twenty seven and losing five. Ellis was a good fighter but the smart money was on Frazier to emerge victorious in this meeting, and the smart money was right. The smart money often is.

Frazier and Ellis become Champions

Frazier continued his winning run when Ellis retired in round four of a scheduled fifteen-round contest. Ellis did not have the firepower to deter Frazier during the course of the fight. He tried all he knew but it had little or no effect on the man with whom he was exchanging punches. Frazer was like an unstoppable tank throwing hurtful punches, the impact of which shook Ellis every time they landed. Frazier was now the undisputed world heavyweight king. This was good for boxing to have the title unified once again, but make no mistake, the large shadow of Muhammed Ali loomed over him. It was evident that Frazier would have to meet and beat Ali to be properly accepted as the true champion of the heavyweight division, despite his win over Ellis, which gave him ownership of the undisputed crown. A super fight between Ali and Frazier looked assured in the future.

Muhammad Ali–Rocky Marciano

When Rocky Marciano retired from boxing he did so having created a record by leaving the sport as the only world heavyweight champion to quit the ring with an undefeated record of forty-nine bouts. That was some feat and one that would be hard to equal by those who would duly follow in the years to come. 'The Rock' was relentless in the ring and would not submit to defeat. Such was his desire to win, Marciano would walk through pain to get the result. He was one hard man and there was just no stopping him, so there was often speculation amongst fans on who would have won had Ali and Marciano met when in their prime. An attempt was made to pacify those who pondered on this when the pair met in a computerised fight. Information about both fighters was duly entered into a computer whereby various different outcomes were presented. When shown, the fight saw Marciano win by a knockout in round thirteen. This result did not please everyone and certainly did not settle any debates between fight pundits on the particular issue. In actual combat, of course, the situation may very well have been different.

Unable to view his victory over Ali

Rocky Marciano was unable to view the computerised contest of himself winning against Muhammad Ali, since he sadly died in a plane crash on

31 August 1969 – one day before his birthday. At the time of his death, Marciano was aged 45 years 11 months and 30 days, having been born on 1 September 1923.

Muhammad Ali's return to the ring

Jerry Quarry became Muhammad Ali's first opponent on his return to the ring on 26 October 1970, after a long absence from boxing due to his refusal to join the US Army. (Ali's last appearance had taken place against Zora Folley on 22 March 1967 at Madison Square Garden, New York, and saw him make a successful defence of the world heavyweight title by way of a seven-round knockout.) Ali's return was a magical moment for boxing. Many fans of the sport wanted to see him back in action. This was big news for the fight game.

There was no doubt that boxing badly needed Ali and Ali badly needed boxing. Quarry represented a stern test for Ali – he entered the contest with a record of forty-five bouts, winning thirty-seven, losing four and drawing four. There were easier options for Ali to have eased his way back into the sport, boxers who would not have been any kind of threat and thus provided him with a surefire win. No one would have criticised Ali had he taken that route in his first fight back. However, he rarely took the easy road during his time in the ring and that was not going to change now. He felt he needed to fight and beat a quality fighter to confirm that he was still one of the best in the division – if not the very best. Ali was raring to go in his quest to get the world heavyweight crown back. Quarry was not a sacrificial goat going to the slaughter – far from it. He was ambitious and was not there to be a showpiece upon whom Ali could display his skills. He was not going to roll over without a fight. A win for Quarry would enhance his reputation, with him being the first man to defeat Ali in the paid ranks. Such a noteworthy victory would certainly open the doors for big money fights in the future.

Quarry's last setback occurred when he was knocked out by George Chuvalo in round seven in a bout scheduled for ten on 12 December 1969 at Madison Square Garden, New York. This was considered something of a shock at the time. He rebounded from that defeat by winning four bouts in succession, the last having taken place on 8 September 1970 against Stamford Harris by way of a six-round stoppage in a bout set for ten at the Auditorium, Miami Beach, Florida.

The venue for the Ali–Quarry contest was the City Auditorium, Atlanta, Georgia. The bout was scheduled for fifteen rounds but didn't go that far as it was stopped in the third stanza. The stoppage came about when Quarry sustained a cut eye, giving Ali the victory he required. It might have been more beneficial for Ali had the fight lasted longer. More rounds would have given him the opportunity to shake off any ring rust that would have accumulated due to him being inactive. However, a win is a win. The former world champion was now undefeated in thirty bouts and had served notice that he was back and ready to make waves once again in the sport.

Chapter 14

Ali Meets with Defeat

Oscar Bonavena beaten by Muhammad Ali

Muhammad Ali was wasting no time in his ring comeback. On 7 December 1970, he met Argentine Oscar Bonavena in a contest scheduled for fifteen rounds. Ali, now undefeated in thirty bouts, was meeting an opponent who had participated in fifty-three bouts, winning forty-six, losing six and drawing one. The bout took place at Madison Square Garden in New York. Bonavena was one tough hombre and would not be tamed easily; he feared no man, including Ali. Bonavena gave everyone he faced a hard time, win or lose. Boxing is often called the 'hurt game', and the Argentine would hurt you, should your concentration lapse at any time during the ring action. The man did not play games. When looking at the situation it had to be wondered if this was the right choice of opponent for Ali at this stage of his comeback. Was he pushing his luck a little, being just a bit too confident? The Jerry Quarry bout was a risk, and so was this one with Bonavena – perhaps even more so.

In his previous bout, on 29 October 1970, Bonavena had battled Luis Faustino Pires of Brazil at the Estadio Luna Park, Buenos Aires, stopping his opponent in round four of ten. When the bell sounded to start the fight with Ali, the man from Argentina went to war in his attempt to get the win, which would be the biggest of his career to date if achieved. The Argentine boxer, as expected, pushed the former world champion hard throughout the bout and was a handful. Ali had to dig deep and could not relax for a moment during the action. The man in front of him was a non-stop punching machine, a tank with no reverse gear. He seemed tireless. However, Ali proved successful and became the first man to legitimately stop the Argentine inside the scheduled distance when he floored his opponent three times in round fifteen, which saw an automatic stoppage. Ali was now ready to step in with the reigning champion, Joe Frazier, in his attempt to regain the world heavyweight crown, which he felt was rightfully his.

Disqualification defeats

Previous to the contest with Muhammad Ali, the only time Oscar Bonavena had been defeated inside the scheduled distance was by a disqualification, on two occasions.

On 12 March 1966 at the Estadio Bristol, Mar del Plata, Buenos Aires, José Giorgetti defeated Bonavena by way of a disqualification in round eight of a scheduled ten. On 10 January 1970, Bonavena suffered the same fate once again when disqualified against opponent Miguel Angel Paez in round seven in a contest set for ten at the Estadio Luna Park, Buenos Aires.

The moment of truth

Muhammad Ali and Joe Frazier met on 8 March 1971 in their much-anticipated world title clash. All the talking was over and it was now time to turn words into action. The eyes of the world would be watching the contest; it had captured the attention of the public in a big way. The fight game was on a new high thanks to the two fighters who were to confront each other. Boxing fans and non-boxing fans alike were looking forward to the encounter. This was the biggest show in town, the show that would answer many questions about the two men facing each other.

After all the speculation and debates, the time had come to clarify who had the right to sit on the world championship throne. This was the moment of truth for both fighters. Ali was bidding to regain the title from the undisputed reigning world heavyweight champion, Frazier. Both fighters entered the ring at Madison Square Garden, New York, with 100 per cent records – Ali with a slate of thirty-one undefeated bouts and Frazier with a perfect twenty-six. Frazier was a proud man and knew he needed to beat Ali to gain the total acceptance amongst boxing fans as the real and rightful champion. Many still considered Ali the true king of the division since he had not lost the title in the ring. This fact must have been irritating for Frazier.

The two men were keen to prove their right to be recognised as the best in their weight category. It was not just the championship at stake in this match but also their pride. As the two fighters entered the ring to duke it out there was a feeling of anticipation amongst the spectators, who felt they were about to witness something very special – an event that would go down in the boxing history books. When the bout began, the two opponents were throwing punches freely inside the square ring, with encouragement from those in attendance. The exciting clash saw both men fight with a steely determination to win and be acclaimed as the true champion at the weight. The defending champion often connected with hard punches to both head and body. Ali retaliated with damaging blows, stinging Frazier with fast jabs. It was obvious that the fighters would feel aches and pains in their bodies in the days that followed. Frazier eventually prevailed in a tough, punishing battle that saw the two combatants give their all in their efforts to win. Ali lost for the first time in the professional ranks after being outpointed over the duration of fifteen rounds. He was also floored for a count by Frazier in the final round, which cemented the defending champion's victory. The loss was a bitter pill for Ali to swallow. It was certain that even before he left the ring, he was plotting his road back to the championship. The meeting was dubbed the 'Fight of the Century' and it truly lived up to that description.

Arthur Mercante Snr

Arthur Mercante Snr was the referee in charge of the Joe Frazier–Muhammad Ali world heavyweight title contest. He had refereed a number of fights over the years and was a most respected official. On this occasion, he became the first man to officiate in a bout that saw Ali lose for the first time in his professional career.

First judges

The judges who sat at the ringside for the Joe Frazier–Muhammad Ali world heavyweight title bout were Artie Aidala and Bill Recht. They became the first judges to score a contest that saw Ali lose for the first time in the professional code.

Muhammad Ali.

Muhammad Ali facing the press in London.

Henry Cooper – the first British fighter to have boxed Muhammad Ali.

Angelo Dundee (left) with Muhammad Ali.

Muhammad Ali and Angelo Dundee share a joke.

Floyd Patterson became the second man to challenge Muhammad Ali for the title.

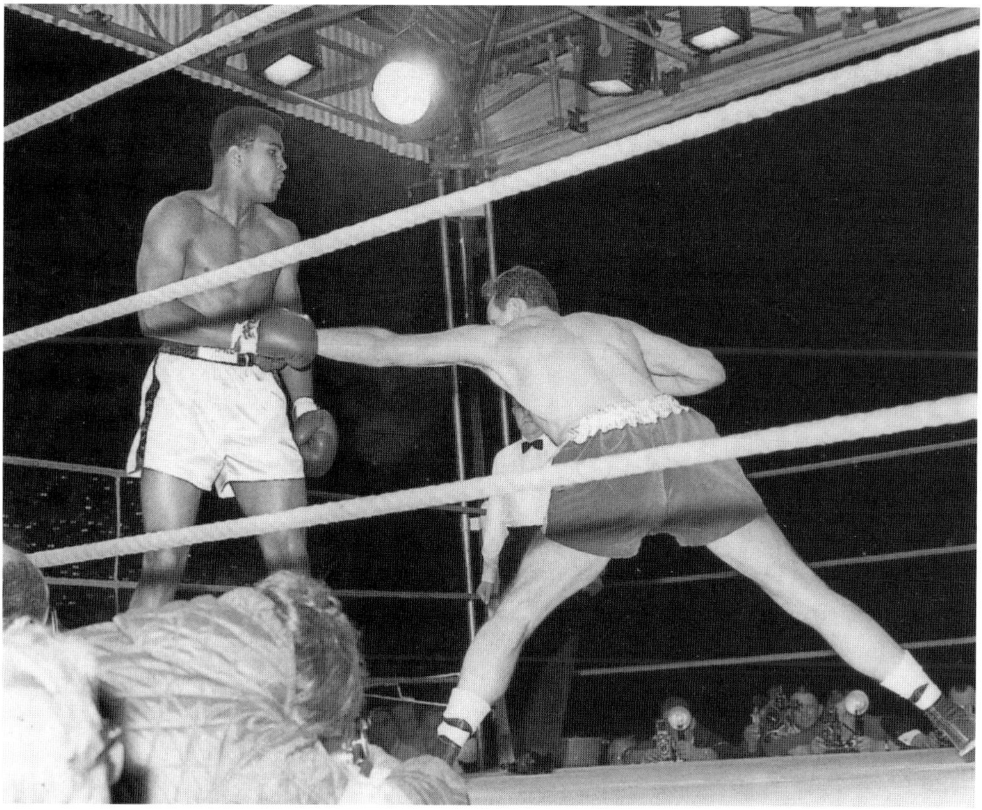

Above: Henry Cooper (right) jabs a left to Ali's body.

Right: Ali (left) poised to defend against a Cooper attack.

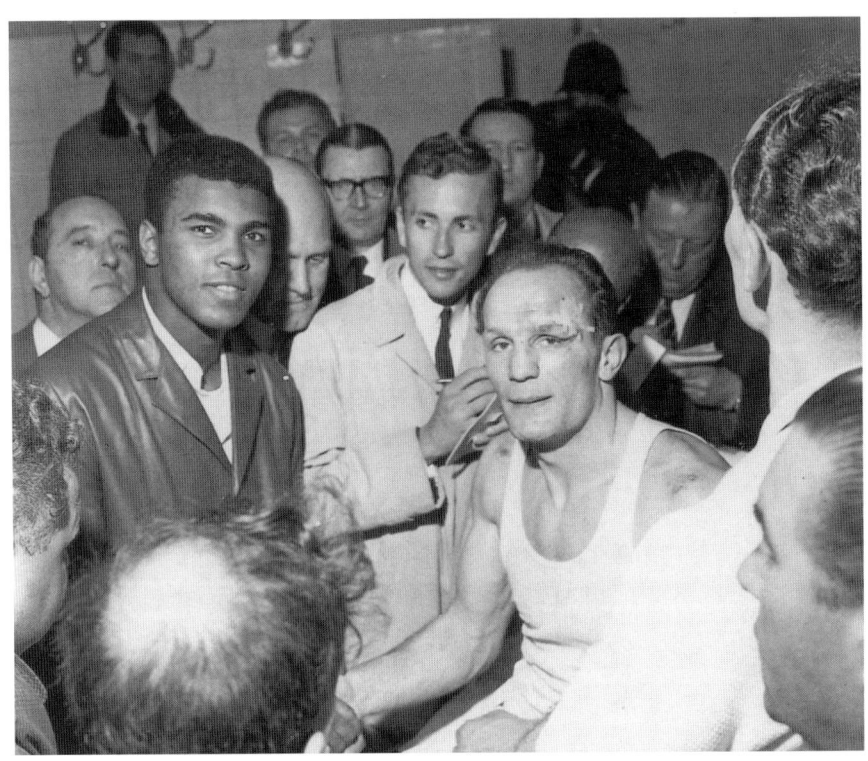

Above: Ali (left) visits Cooper after fight.

Below: Ali looks on while George Smith checks Cooper's cut eye.

Henry Cooper – the first boxer to be knighted. (*Philip Sharkey*)

Henry Cooper with his three Lonsdale belts.

Angelo Dundee (left) checks the wraps on Ali's hands.

Left: Muhammad Ali takes in the sights of London while he is in town.

Below: Actor David Prowse (left), promoter Alex Steene and Muhammad Ali.

Above: Boxing journalist and commentator Reg Gutteridge (left) with Teddy Waltham.

Below: Muhammad Ali (left) with Angelo Dundee.

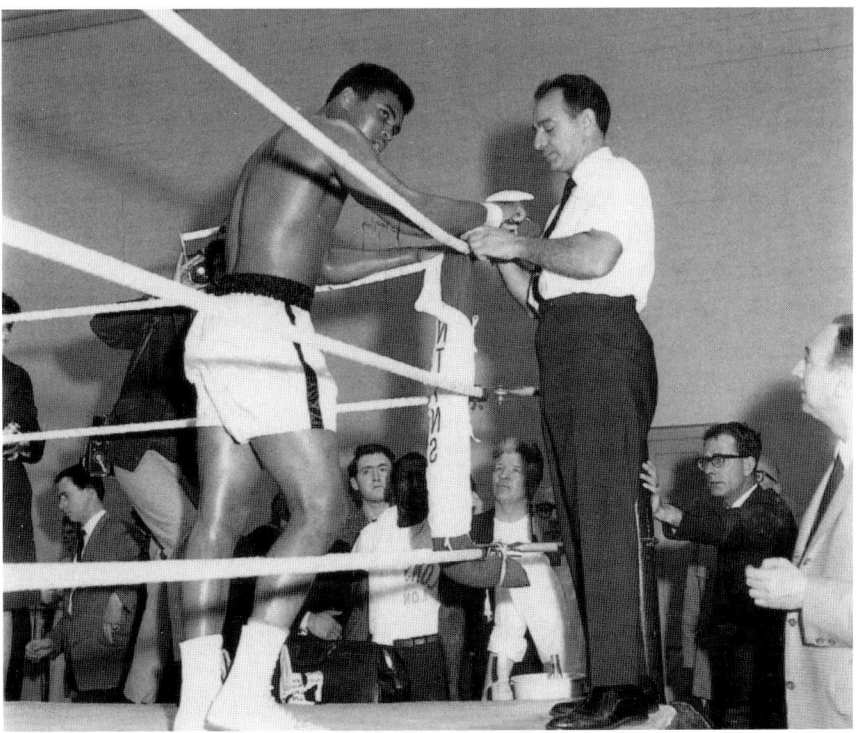

Above: Joe Frazier – the first man to defeat Muhammad Ali in professional ranks.

Below: Former world heavyweight champion Jack Dempsey (left) and Danny McAlinden (centre) with former world light-heavyweight king, Georges Carpentier.

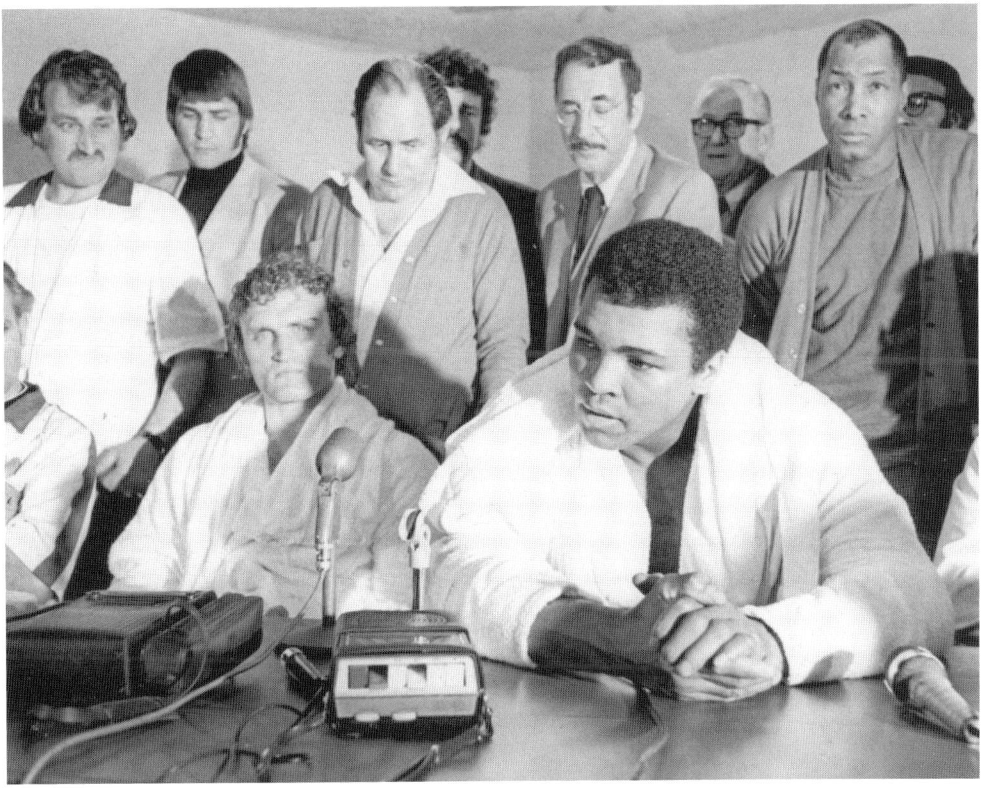

Above: Joe Bugner (left) in a press conference with Muhammad Ali after their contest.

Right: George Foreman (left) with promoter Jack Solomons.

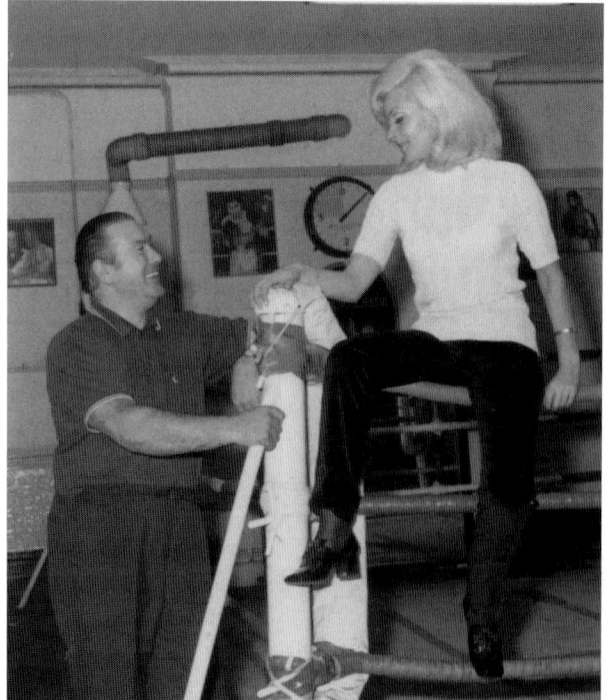

Above: Joe Bugner fought in front of Muhammad Ali when the champion was in London.

Left: Boxing promoter Beryl Cameron-Gibbons asked Ali a question on the TV show *An Audience with Muhammad Ali*. Danny Holland is on the left.

Joe Bugner failed to win the world heavyweight title.

Billy Aird held Jimmy Young to a draw.

Right: Richard Dunn – first British heavyweight challenger with the southpaw stance to fight for the world heavyweight title.

Below: Muhammad Ali, a frequent visitor to the UK, met future IBF world cruiserweight champion Glenn McCrory (left).

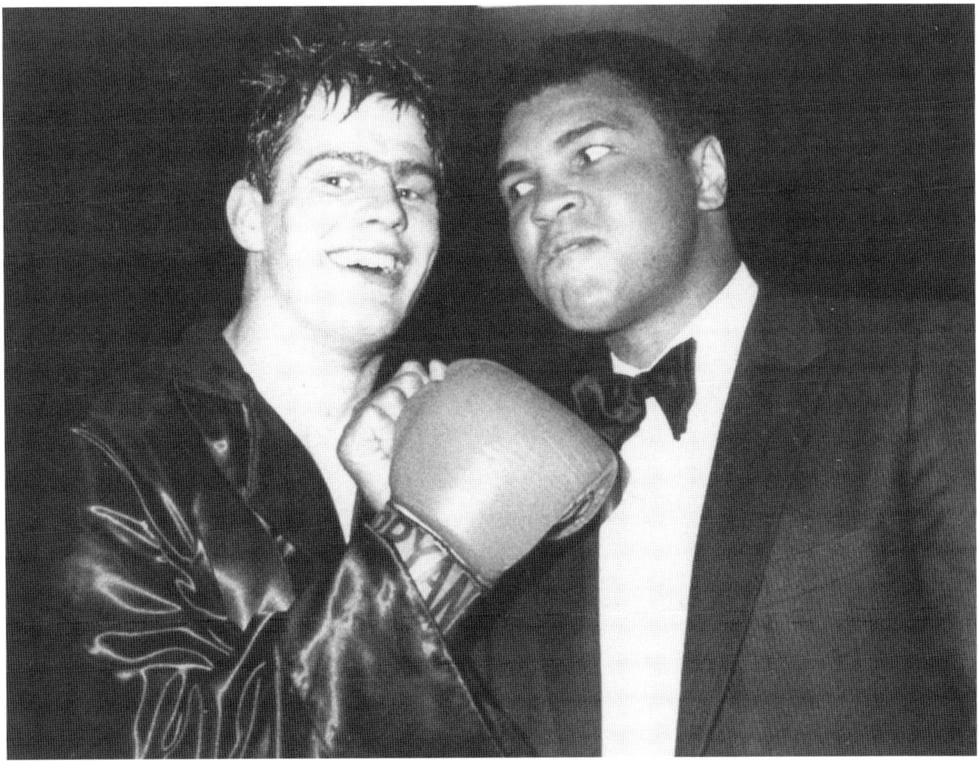

Above: Muhammad Ali (left), Sammy Davis Jr. (centre) and Drew Bundini Brown.

Left: Muhammad Ali fought the very best during his career.

All images, unless otherwise specified, courtesy of Derek Rowe.

Ali Meets with Defeat

Old Blue Eyes

We all know that Frank Sinatra was pretty good when it came to singing and acting. In fact, without question he was one of the very best – a true legend in the entertainment industry. He was also a very keen boxing fan. At the age of 55 years, 2 months and 24 days, he became an accredited press photographer. The aim of this new vocation was that he could be at the ringside to take some action shots of the Joe Frazier–Muhammad Ali world heavyweight title clash. What do you know – Old Blue Eyes was pretty good at this too. It seemed his talents knew no bounds. One of his photographs even appeared on the front cover of *Life* magazine.

The twelfth former world champion

When Muhammad Ali lost in his bid to regain the world heavyweight title from Joe Frazier he became the twelfth fighter to do so. Previous former champions who failed to recapture the crown they once held were: James J. Corbett, Bob Fitzsimmons, James J. Jeffries, Jack Dempsey, Max Schmeling, Joe Louis, Ezzard Charles, Jersey Joe Walcott, Ingemar Johansson, Floyd Patterson and Sonny Liston. (Please note: Floyd Patterson did, of course, regain the championship from Ingemar Johansson in 1960 but he failed in three other attempts when challenging Sonny Liston 1963, Muhammad Ali, 1965, and Jimmy Ellis, 1968, for the title.)

Two undefeated Olympic gold medal winners

Muhammad Ali and Joe Frazier became the first former Olympic gold medal winners with an undefeated professional record to contest the world heavyweight championship.

Bad night for the Ali family

It really proved to be a bad night for the Ali family. On the same card as the Joe Frazier–Muhammad Ali world heavyweight title bout, Northern

Ireland's Danny McAlinden, who came into the ring with a record consisting of seventeen fights, winning fourteen, with one defeat and two drawn, outpointed Muhammad Ali's brother, Rahman Ali, over six rounds. Rahman, like his older brother, lost his undefeated record, which had previously stood at seven. Ali pushed on with his career after his defeat by McAlinden, taking part in a further ten bouts, winning seven, losing two and drawing one. His final contest took place on 13 September 1972 in San Diego, California, where he was knocked out in the eighth round of ten by Jack O'Halloran.

Danny McAlinden makes history

Following his victory over Rahman Ali, Danny McAlinden returned to the UK and went on to create a record of his own when he became the first Irish boxer to win the British & Commonwealth heavyweight championship. This event took place on 27 June 1972, when McAlinden knocked out defending title holder Jack Bodell in two rounds in a scheduled fifteen at Villa Park, Birmingham.

Chapter 15

Ali Captures the NABF Title

Angelo Dundee in opposite corner

It could be said that Muhammad Ali was taking a risk and embarking on a dangerous route when, on 26 July 1971, he fought former WBA heavyweight king Jimmy Ellis at the Astrodome in Houston, Texas. This was Ali's first bout since losing to Joe Frazier in his bid to regain the undisputed world heavyweight title. Ellis came to the party with a resume of thirty-six bouts, winning thirty and losing six.

Last time out, Ellis had a good win when he outpointed George Chuvalo over ten rounds on 10 May 1971 at the Maple Leaf Gardens, Toronto. The risk to Ali was that on this occasion, his trainer, Angelo Dundee, was in Ellis's corner. Dundee obviously knew Ali's strengths and weaknesses, which was clearly an advantage for Ellis. Ellis was also a stablemate of Ali's and had sparred many rounds with him over the years. He too would be aware of any flaws the former undisputed world heavyweight champion may have had and exploit them fully during the bout. Nevertheless, despite these factors, Ali emerged victorious. He won when he stopped Ellis in the twelfth and final round to win the vacant NABF heavyweight title and took a step towards another possible crack at the world heavyweight championship. Ali's resume now stood at thirty-two wins, with one defeat.

Previous NABF title holder

The previous holder of the NABF championship prior to the Muhammad Ali–Jimmy Ellis contest was Leotis Martin, who won the crown on 6 December 1969. Martin won the title when knocking out an opponent well known to Muhammad Ali – the former world heavyweight king,

Sonny Liston. Martin closed the show in fine style in the ninth session in a contest set for twelve. The contest was for the inaugural title. The venue for the Martin–Liston fight was the International Hotel and Casino in Las Vegas. Martin later retired from the sport, reportedly due to a detached retina, which he had sustained during his contest with Liston.

First defence of NABF heavyweight title

Muhammad Ali entered the ring at the Astrodome in Houston, Texas, on 17 November 1971 to make the first defence of his NABF heavyweight title. In the opposing corner was Buster Mathis, who came to the contest with a resume of thirty-one professional bouts, with just two defeats. The first loss came at the hands of Joe Frazier on 4 March 1968, when stopped in round eleven of fifteen. On that occasion, he was contesting the vacant NYSAC world heavyweight title at Madison Square Garden, New York. Then, prior to meeting Ali, Mathis lost a twelve-round points decision to Jerry Quarry in a bout that took place on 24 March 1969, the venue once again being Madison Square Garden.

This latest engagement for Mathis looked like another certain defeat for him unless he could raise the bar and pull off an incredible victory. There was no doubting the fact that Mathis needed a win to breathe new life into his career. Ali climbed between the ropes with a slate of thirty-two wins, with one defeat. The fight went the full distance of twelve rounds and it was no shock when Ali added another victory to his win column with a points victory. Mathis was floored twice in round eleven and twice in round twelve by the former world heavyweight champion.

First to box in Switzerland

On 26 December 1971, Muhammad Ali paid a visit to Switzerland. It wasn't to admire the scenic views, or for yodelling lessons or to hear tales about William Tell – it was for business. He was to meet Germany's future European heavyweight champion Jürgen Blin, who had a resume of forty-two bouts, winning twenty-seven and losing nine, with six drawn. Ali had a record of thirty-four bouts, with just one defeat.

Ali Captures the NABF Title

In his last bout, on 1 October 1971, Blin had taken care of opponent George Johnson by a stoppage in two rounds in a bout set for ten in a fight that had taken place in Hamburg, Germany. There was only going to be one winner in this contest and – when looking at the fighting history of both men – that, of course, had to be Ali. No one felt that Blin was going to turn the form book upside down and win. Upsets do happen in boxing, but it was not likely on this night. The fight had actually been arranged to keep Ali busy. Blin wanted to prove the critics wrong and show that he was not just fodder for Ali. Here was a chance for him to make a name for himself and crash the ratings with an unexpected win. Brave as he was, the German did not have the ring skills to take a victory against the American. Blin pushed forward during the bout but he became predicable as the rounds passed by, and was an easy target for Ali to land his punches on. The former world heavyweight king ended the bout when the contest was stopped in the seventh round of a bout scheduled for twelve. The venue for the bout was the Hallenstadion, Zürich. Ali became the first former world heavyweight champion from the USA to box in Switzerland.

Back in Europe

The bout against Jürgen Blin saw Muhammad Ali box for the first time since 10 September 1966 in a European country. On that occasion, Ali defended his WBC world heavyweight crown against yet another German opponent, Karl Mildenberger, who was stopped in the twelfth stanza in a contest set for the duration of fifteen rounds. The contest took place in Waldstadion/Radrennbahn, Frankfurt.

Jack Johnson – an historical note

On the same date as the Muhammad Ali–Jürgen Blin bout, but way back in 1908, Jack Johnson from the USA rocked the world big time. He became the first black boxer to win the world heavyweight championship, when he halted the defending title holder, Tommy Burns of Canada, in round fourteen of twenty. The contest took place at the Sydney Stadium, New South Wales, Australia. Johnson eventually lost the championship to

Jess Willard on 5 April 1915 by a knockout in the twenty-sixth round of a scheduled forty-five. The venue for the Johnson–Willard bout was the Oriental Park in Havana, Cuba.

Boxing in Japan

Over the years, Japan has produced a number of world champions in various weight divisions but had yet to produce a world heavyweight champion, or indeed a serious contender in the division. So seeing a former heavyweight title holder in action must have been a special event for the Japanese fans. Muhammad Ali was booked to fight in front of them at the Nippon Budokan, Tokyo, a venue that had staged many fights over the years. On 1 April 1972, Ali took to the ring and outpointed opponent Mac Foster over the duration of fifteen rounds. The bout was not one that could be called epic in any way. Ali got the job done without being troubled and was ready to march on to the next assignment.

Foster came into the contest with an impressive record of twenty-nine bouts, with twenty-eight victories and one defeat. The loss came at the hands of Jerry Quarry on 17 June 1970, at Madison Square Garden, New York. Lewis was stopped in round six of ten. Since the loss to Quarry, Foster had rebuilt his career, winning his next four fights in succession. His last bout had taken place on 26 December 1971 against Italian Giuseppe Ros, whom he defeated by knocking him out in round eight of ten. The venue was the Hallenstadion, Zürich (on the undercard of the Ali–Blin bout). This made him an acceptable opponent for Ali to meet in Japan. Ali went into the fight with Foster with a resume of thirty-five bouts, with one defeat. The contest saw Ali go the full distance of fifteen rounds for the first time outside of a world title contest.

Japanese heavyweight champion

At the time of the Muhammad Ali–Mac Foster fight, the Japanese heavyweight title was vacant. The first boxer to have held the national championship at the poundage was Noboru Kataoka, who had won the vacant crown on 4 May 1957, outpointing Yutaka Nakagoshi over ten rounds at the Kyobashi Hall, Tokyo. Kataoka later retired from boxing without defending the crown.

Ali Captures the NABF Title

A return to Canada

In a world title defence on 29 March 1966, Muhammad Ali had successfully defended his WBC world heavyweight crown against George Chuvalo in a contest that went the full distance of fifteen rounds. Once again, Chuvalo was in the challenger's corner, attempting this time to rip the NABF heavyweight title away from Ali's grasp. It would, of course, have been nice to have won the title but the bigger prize in this fight for Chuvalo was the possibility of a victory over Ali. That was the major goal for the Canadian – to be just the second man in the professional ranks to defeat Ali. Now that would be something.

Chuvalo's last defeat had taken place on 10 May 1971 against former WBA heavyweight king Jimmy Ellis at the Maple Leaf Gardens in Toronto, by way of a ten-round points decision. Since that setback, Chuvalo had bounced back and won three bouts in succession. His last fight was against Jim Christopher on 21 February 1972 at the Winnipeg Arena, Manitoba, which saw him win by a knockout in two rounds of a scheduled ten. The Ali–Chuvalo bout took place at the Pacific Coliseum, Vancouver, British Columbia, on 1 May 1972. Even with the home fans fully behind him, the Canadian was unable to get the better of the American, whose boxing skills were far superior. Chuvalo always gave his best, throwing punches until the very end. He was a real fighting man who would walk through both pain and punishment to get to his opponent. Chuvalo would never accept that quitting was an option. It was not an easy night's work for Ali but he was always one if not two steps ahead of the Canadian during the hectic battle. Consequently, Ali retained his title on points over twelve rounds. He had entered the ring with a slate of thirty-six fights, with one defeat, whilst Chuvalo had a resume of eighty-five fights, winning sixty-six and losing seventeen, with two drawn.

Jerry Quarry – 2

On 27 June 1972, Muhammad Ali and Jerry Quarry met for the second time. The venue for the contest was the Convention Center, Las Vegas. Quarry had been the opponent to test Ali on his return to the ring after his exile from the sport. On that occasion, Ali won by a three-round cut-eye stoppage. Quarry was far from pleased with the result. Like all true fighters, Quarry had the heart of a warrior and felt that he could have won the bout had it not been for the injury. Since their previous meeting, Quarry had fought on six occasions, all bouts resulting in a win. His last outing had taken place on 9 May 1972, and saw him put in a workmanlike performance to outpoint Larry Middleton over ten rounds. The bout had taken place at the Empire Pool, Wembley. Quarry's resume was now standing at fifty-two fights, comprising forty-three wins and five defeats, with four drawn. Ali too had been active since last meeting Quarry, boxing on seven occasions, bringing his record up to thirty-seven fights, with one defeat.

Quarry was fully intent on giving Ali his second defeat in the paid ranks. Before the fight started, heavyweight contender George Foreman was introduced into the ring and was obviously watching both fighters with professional interest. Ali was defending his NABF heavyweight title, which he successfully retained for the third time when he stopped Quarry in round seven of twelve, leaving no room for doubt about who was the better fighter.

At the start of the contest, Quarry attacked furiously, forcing Ali back onto the ropes, but the former world heavyweight king weathered the storm. Ali was untroubled and started to take control as the fight wore on, punishing his opponent at every opportunity. Ali was looking good, up on his toes and moving around the ring, popping out his left jab into Quarry's face. It was a case of onwards and upwards for Ali.

Younger brother of Jerry Quarry

On the same card as the Muhammad Ali–Jerry Quarry contest, a world light-heavyweight title fight took place. The defending champion, Bob Foster, retained his undisputed crown when he knocked out Mike Quarry in the fourth round of a scheduled fifteen. Quarry was the younger brother of Jerry. It was a very bad night for the Quarry family. Foster would meet Ali in a future contest.

Chapter 16

Defeated for a Second Time

A visit to Ireland

The much-travelled Muhammad Ali made his first professional appearance in Ireland on 19 July 1972 at Croke Park in Dublin. His opponent, Al (Blue) Lewis, also from the USA, found that the luck of the Irish did not rub off on him since he was stopped in round eleven of a bout scheduled for twelve. Going into the contest Lewis had a record of thirty fights, winning twenty-six and losing four. Ali had a ledger of thirty-eight bouts, with just the one defeat. Lewis was as game as they come and gave it his best shot, knowing of course that should he be able to become the second man to beat Ali, many doors would be open for him. He would be the new star in boxing.

In his last bout, Lewis had travelled to Argentina to meet the very tough Oscar Bonavena. The pair met at the Estadio Luna Park, Buenos Aires. The chances of Lewis returning to the states with a victory under his belt were remote but you had to give the American full respect for taking this risky contest. The fight did not go well for Lewis against Bonavena since it ended with him being disqualified in round seven of ten.

A win against Ali did not look to be on the cards. Lewis may well have thought he had a plan to beat the former world heavyweight king when going into the fight. However, like so many of Ali's previous opponents, it was easier to think about beating Ali than actually do the deed. To his credit, Lewis had his moments during the fight but those moments soon passed. Lewis found that he was not able to overcome the skills of the former world heavyweight title holder.

Muhammad Ali: The Man Who Changed Boxing

Floyd Patterson's last professional contest

On 20 September 1972, Muhammad Ali took to the ring once again to make a fourth defence of his NABF heavyweight title. His challenger was former two-time heavyweight title holder Floyd Patterson. The two protagonists had previously crossed gloves on 22 November 1965. On that occasion, Patterson challenged Ali for the WBC version of the heavyweight title and was thus defeated in emphatic fashion, being stopped in round twelve of fifteen. Since their first meeting, Patterson had fought on fifteen occasions, winning twelve, losing two and drawing one of his bouts. His last defeat had taken place on 14 September 1968, when he was outpointed by Jimmy Ellis over fifteen rounds when attempting to win the WBA world heavyweight belt in a contest that took place in Sweden, the venue being the Rasunda Fotbollsstadion in Stockholm.

Patterson's last foray in the ring had taken place on 14 July 1972. The outing saw Patterson exchange punches with Pedro Agosto at the Singer Bowl, Flushing Meadows, Queens, New York. It was a successful night for Patterson since he won by a stoppage in six rounds of a bout scheduled for ten. Patterson's resume now stood at sixty-three bouts, winning fifty-five and losing seven, with one drawn. Ali entered the fray against Patterson armed with a record of thirty-nine bouts, with just one defeat. Since his first clash with Patterson, Ali had fought seventeen times, losing on just the one well-publicised occasion to Joe Frazier when bidding to regain the world title. It did not seem likely that Patterson would be able to reverse his previous defeat to Ali. The bout, which took place at Madison Square Garden, New York, saw Ali once again prove his supremacy over his opponent, who retired in round seven of twelve. Consequently, Ali became the last man to box Patterson since the former two-time world heavyweight king retired from the ring soon after the defeat. Ali's record now stood at forty fights, with one defeat.

Cut for the first time

On 21 November 1972, Muhammad Ali made the fifth defence of the NABF heavyweight title against the reigning world light-heavyweight king Bob Foster, who had a record of fifty-four bouts, comprising forty-nine wins, with five defeats.

Defeated for a Second Time

Foster had challenged Joe Frazier for the world heavyweight title on 18 November 1970 at the Cobo Arena, Detroit, and was knocked out in round two of a contest that was made for the duration of fifteen. You did not have to be a fight expert to realise that the bout with Ali was clearly not going to go the full distance. Ali came into the fight to face Foster with a record of forty bouts, with one defeat. Ali was never in danger of losing to his challenger. Foster was a great champion at light-heavyweight, there was no doubt about that; it was the poundage where he truly excelled. Prior to his bout with Ali, Foster had successfully defended his title on 26 September 1972 at the Empire Pool, Wembley, against the reigning British, European and Commonwealth champion Chris Finnegan. Foster won by a knockout in round fourteen of fifteen. Foster had dynamite in his fists but the higher division was too much for him.

It is often said in boxing that 'a good big 'un will always beat a good small 'un'. Like everything in life, there is of course always the exception to the rule, but not on this occasion. Ali was in control from the first bell, thus dominating the proceedings. Foster made a fight of it and did land his share of punches on Ali before the end came, but they were not enough to deter him. Foster was floored seven times during the fight – four times in the fifth round, twice in the seventh and once in the eighth. Ali retained the crown with a knockout in round eight of a scheduled twelve, the venue for the fight being the Sahara Tahoe Hotel, Stateline, Nevada. While Foster did not achieve a sensational win by beating Ali, he did gain a degree of satisfaction by becoming the first fighter to cut Ali in the professional ranks. Ali sustained an injury over the left eye in the fifth round.

A future headache

On the undercard of the Muhammad Ali–Bob Foster contest was a bout between Ken Norton and Henry Clark. Norton came into the bout with a resume of twenty-eight contests, winning twenty-seven, with one defeat. Clark came in with a record consisting of thirty-four fights, with twenty-four wins and seven defeats, with three drawn. Norton won his bout when he knocked out Clark in round nine of a scheduled ten. There wasn't anything outstanding about the contest, really nothing to get too excited about. The fight was not exactly a headline grabber, just two good heavyweights going through their paces to earn their bread in the hope that a win would get them involved in bigger bouts. That being said, few of the spectators watching the contest at the time realised that Norton would prove to be one big headache for Ali in the very near future – one he could well have done without.

First British opponent since Brian London

On 14 February 1973, Muhammad Ali met his first British opponent since Brian London, whom he had knocked out in the third of a fifteen-round contest on 6 August 1966, when defending his WBC world heavyweight crown. On this outing, Ali was facing Joe Bugner, the reigning European and former British and Commonwealth title holder, who had a resume of forty-eight bouts, winning forty-three, losing four, with one drawn.

Bugner was considered in the UK to have potential and it was hoped that he just might, in due course, join the ranks of the heavyweight elites. The contest, which took place at the Convention Center, Las Vegas, saw Ali enter the ring with a slate of forty-one fights, losing just once. Truthfully, the fight was not overly exciting. Bugner was not able to get the best of the former world heavyweight king at any time during the bout. Did anyone really think that Bugner would win against a man of Ali's stature? Not really. At best, the contest was going to add to the young Briton's boxing education, giving him rounds with an exceptional fighter. Bugner was durable and wasn't likely to be stopped by Ali. Had Bugner somehow got lucky and won, well that would have been a stunner, a bonus to his career. So there was no real gasp of astonishment at the result. The fight went very much as expected. Ali was too ringwise for his opponent and thus increased his win ratio when he boxed his way to a twelve-round points victory over Bugner.

From Elvis Presley

Muhammad Ali entered the ring to face Joe Bugner wearing a robe with the words 'People's Choice' embroidered on the back. The robe had been given to Ali by singer Elvis Presley, king of rock 'n' roll. Ali may well have been 'all shook up' by the generous gift but at no time was he shook up by Joe Bugner's punches during their contest.

Larry Holmes's professional debut

On 21 March 1973, Larry Holmes made his professional debut at the Catholic Youth Center, Scranton, Pennsylvania. Holmes showed his potential and outpointed his opponent, Rodell Dupree, over four rounds. In the fullness of time, Holmes would not only go on to become an outstanding world heavyweight champion but also prove to feature in the career of Muhammad Ali.

Second boxer to defeat Ali

To use a familiar expression: no one saw that one coming. On 31 March 1973, Muhammad Ali faced Ken Norton at the Sports Arena, San Diego, in a defence of his NABF heavyweight crown. Norton was a good fighter with a record comprising thirty bouts, with just one loss, the said defeat having taken place on 2 July 1970 in fight number seventeen at the Olympic Auditorium, Los Angeles. It was José Luis Garcia from Venezuela who spoilt Norton's undefeated record by way of a knockout in round eight of ten. This was a disappointment for Norton but he was able to shake off the loss and put together thirteen wins. This included a ten-round points decision victory over Charlie Reno in San Diego, California, on 13 December 1972 – a fight he won before getting between the ropes to face Ali.

Few if any gave Norton any kind of a chance of defeating Ali. The general feeling was that Norton was good but not special. The former world champion had a resume of forty-two contests, with just the one defeat. The bout would see Ali victorious, taking him that vital step nearer to a second chance of regaining the world crown. Well, that appeared to be the plan prior to the contest. Norton had plans of his own; he was ambitious and wanted a taste of the big time. He wanted to be a major player and Ali was his ticket to achieve his aspirations. On the night, Norton upped his game and surprised the boxing world when he defeated Ali on a points decision over the twelve-round duration to become just the second man to defeat Ali in the professional ranks. Ali left the ring with a resume of forty-three bouts, with two defeats.

Broken jaw

During the course of his contest with Ken Norton, Muhammad Ali sustained a broken jaw. Despite this injury, Ali bravely continued to fight on until the final bell rang. Considering the magnitude of the injury Ali suffered, no one would have condemned him had he looked for the way out and quit during the fight. The pain must have been unbearable as he continued the bout, the kind of pain that might well have persuaded many other fighters to exit the fight rather than risk taking more punches to the injury. This was further confirmation that Ali had the courage to go alongside his extensive boxing skills. However, many had now started to wonder if the cracks were starting to show. Was this the beginning of the end for Ali? Some critics were doubtful that he would ever be able to climb back to the top. Was the party over?

Operation

After his shock defeat to Ken Norton, Muhammad Ali was taken to San Diego's Claremont Hospital, where Dr Gary Manchester operated successfully on his broken jaw. The procedure took a reported ninety minutes to perform, which gives an indication of just how serious was Ali's injury.

Chapter 17

Ali Regains World Heavyweight Title

Revenge

It was crucial for Muhammad Ali to gain revenge over his previous conqueror, Ken Norton, in their return contest on 10 September 1973. The bout took place at The Forum, Inglewood, California. Since their last meeting, neither man had engaged in another bout. Norton now had a record of thirty-one bouts, with one defeat, and Ali had a resume of forty-one victories, with two defeats. There was a great deal at stake in this bout for both men. Should Ali lose again it would bring to an end to his chances of landing a second shot at the world title. There was no way to circumnavigate the fact that Ali had to win this fight. Should Norton defeat Ali for a second time, it would put him very much in the forefront of challengers for the title, thus confirming his status as a genuine contender with all the rewards that would surely follow.

After defeating Ali once, Norton was more than confident that he would do so again, and in doing so, retain the NABF title, which was also on the line. There was no doubt that Norton felt he had the measure of the man he was confronting and that the outcome would be the same as their first meeting. Norton looked more than ready to go to war and give it everything he had. Ali was more than keen to oblige. It was a very tough contest, which was nip and tuck all the way. Ali extracted revenge when he outpointed Norton over the scheduled twelve rounds to keep his hopes of another world title opportunity very much alive. Both Ali and his team were clearly relieved when the decision was announced at the conclusion of the fight. They were aware that it had been a close fight.

First to regain NABF heavyweight title

Defeating Ken Norton was, of course, Muhammad Ali's main priority in their bout. Everything was riding on a victory; a loss in this contest would have been a disaster for the former world heavyweight champion. However, it is also worth noting that Ali not only reversed his previous defeat in this contest but he also became the first boxer to regain the NABF heavyweight crown.

Norton gets a crack at Foreman

Despite the defeat at the hands of Muhammad Ali, it was Ken Norton who actually challenged next for the world title and not his victor. Such are the strange ways of boxing. On 26 March 1974, Norton stepped in with the reigning heavyweight world heavyweight champion George Foreman, who was undefeated in thirty-nine bouts and would be making the second defence of the crown against him.

The venue for the fight was El Poliedro in Caracas, Venezuela. Foreman was the favourite to remain champion. It was difficult to tip against the man – he looked unbeatable. Yet after his strong showings against Ali, it looked as if Norton would give Foreman a competitive night, giving him his hardest fight to date – perhaps even pushing him all the way. Norton was after all an accomplished and polished performer, a man who was more than capable. That did not prove to be the case: the frightening power unleashed by the champion crushed Norton in two rounds. The fight never looked like going the full distance of fifteen rounds.

An easy outing in Indonesia

On 20 October 1973, Muhammad Ali paid a visit to Indonesia to box Rudi Lubbers from The Netherlands. The opponent Ali was facing had a record of twenty-two fights, winning twenty-one and losing one. The said defeat came against Joe Bugner on 16 January 1973, when challenging for the European heavyweight crown at the Royal Albert Hall, Kensington, London. Lubbers duly lost a fifteen-round points decision to the Briton.

Ali Regains World Heavyweight Title

Ali came into the contest against Lubbers with a resume of forty-four bouts, winning forty-two, with two defeats. A win over Lubbers by Ali would prove very little in the world of boxing. By contrast, a win over Ali by Lubbers would shake the foundations of the sport to its very core. Frankly, that was never going to happen – not in a million years.

In his defeat against Bugner, it was apparent that Lubbers did not have the skills or the firepower to defeat a man of Ali's class. It looked a very easy night's work for Ali – indeed, a stroll in the park. Some critics may have been critical about Ali participating in what was perceived to be such a pointless fight. However, with the best will in the world, it must be said that after two very demanding bouts with Ken Norton, Ali deserved to have a fight that wasn't going to be too testing. He really did not need an opponent who was going to take him down to the wire this time around. After twelve rounds of boxing at the Bung Karno Stadium, Jakarta, Ali emerged victorious when he breezed his way to a clear points victory in what was, as expected, an easy outing for him – an ideal tune-up before he tackled more highly ranked opposition in the months to come.

Muhammad Ali–Joe Frazier 2

Muhammad Ali had the opportunity to gain revenge over yet another opponent. This time, the target was the first man to defeat him in the professional ranks – Joe Frazier. The loss came when he challenged Frazier for the world heavyweight crown on 8 March 1971. Frazier was now a former world champion, having lost his title to George Foreman in an upset that took place on 22 January 1973. Despite Frazier's loss to Foreman, the fight with Ali was still an enticing prospect. Frazier had returned to his winning ways on 2 July 1973, when he took on Joe Bugner in a twelve-round bout at the Earls Court Arena, Kensington, London. Frazier came through with a points decision, which opened up the door for the return bout with Ali.

On the night, Ali entered the battle with a record of forty-five bouts, winning forty-three and losing two, whilst Frazier's resume stood at thirty-one bouts, with one defeat. Like their first encounter, the venue for the return was Madison Square Garden, New York. The battle saw Ali put the NABF heavyweight crown on the line for the first time in his second reign. Frazier needed to prove that he was still very relevant in the division and defeating Ali again would more than confirm this. It would surely put him back in the running for another world championship chance. Truth be told, both men needed the victory to keep their hopes alive for a world title chance in the future.

The fight, which took place on 28 January 1974, saw Ali win with a twelve-round points victory. The fight, whilst interesting, did not live up to their previous epic encounter; it lacked the drama and intensity. However, let's be clear: it was still a good contest between two skilful exponents of the sport. Expecting another war between the two was really too much to hope for. The win over Frazier took Ali a step closer to the reigning world heavyweight champion, George Foreman.

TV brawl

Prior to their second meeting in the ring, former world heavyweight champion Muhammad Ali met Joe Frazier on the *Wide World of Sports* TV show. The programme saw Howard Cosell interview the two fighters about their forthcoming encounter. Also on the agenda was a conversation about their past meeting, which had seen Ali fail to regain the championship, which was then held by Frazier. The debate soon heated up, resulting in a brawl in the TV studio. This may have excited the viewers watching at home but the spectacle did not please the boxing authorities.

Not a chance

Muhammad Ali had over the years produced performances that had defied logic, often achieving what seemed to be the impossible. Ali had made a habit of shocking the critics who had tipped against him, often writing him off without a hope. It looked as if those predicting his doom on this occasion might well be right. This time, his challenge against the reigning world heavyweight champion, George Foreman, looked one step too far, even for Ali.

Foreman was the man who had ripped the title from Joe Frazier on 22 January 1973 at the National Stadium, Kingston, Jamaica,

Ali Regains World Heavyweight Title

with frightening ease, stopping the then undefeated champion in two rounds of a scheduled fifteen. In his first defence after the Frazier victory, Foreman knocked out José Roman in one round at the Nippon, Budokan, Tokyo, on 1 September 1973. The fight was set for the championship distance of fifteen rounds. That was very optimistic, to say the least, since Foreman was levels above Roman in both ability and punching power. A trip to El Poliedro, Caracas, Venezuela, later followed, which saw Foreman dismantle Ken Norton easily in two rounds in his second defence of the crown. This bout took place on 26 March 1974. It was an impressive victory, since Norton was a class act. It now appeared that no one was capable of lasting fifteen rounds with the champion, who was looking better and stronger in every bout. To say the reigning title holder was dangerous was an understatement: he looked unbeatable. Foreman looked capable of being the champion for a number of years. There was no one on the horizon who looked to have even a remote chance of taking the title from him. His punching power was undeniable. He was undefeated in forty bouts and had stopped or knocked out thirty-seven of his previous opponents. There should have been a warning put out that fighting Foreman was bad for your health: 'Keep away, you've been warned.' Any mistakes made by Ali in this contest would surely see him get punished badly by the champion.

The general opinion of the experts was that Foreman would retain his crown inside the distance. Ali was not the fighter of old; his cloak of invincibility had been stripped from him with his defeats to Joe Frazier and Ken Norton. He was no longer the ring's Superman. His time was over; his time was done. Foreman would show Ali that a new era had arrived in boxing and the exit door was wide open for him to depart. When considering the facts, it was difficult to argue with that point of view, which many a respected sports journalist held prior to their meeting. Ali, as always, was confident of victory and showed no fear of the man who would be standing in front of him on the night. He clearly felt he had the ability to beat Foreman and would take the title.

The contest took place on 30 October 1974 at the Stade du 20, Mai, Kinshasa, Democratic Republic of the Congo. Once again, Ali proved the doubters wrong and showed that he still had a great deal to offer the sport. In the early stages of the contest, he scored with some stinging jabs and used his footwork in his attempt to avoid some of Foreman's damaging punches. It looked only a matter of time before Foreman would close the show and take out Ali with one of his booming blows. The fight was obviously not going the full distance of fifteen rounds. The end would come sooner rather than later, with a Foreman victory. The bout came to a conclusion in round eight, when it was the challenger who knocked out a clearly exhausted Foreman. Ali was back at the top, the main man once more. The whole world was shocked once again by Ali, as indeed Foreman must have been by the result. The fight was called the 'Rumble in the Jungle'.

The sport now took on a new lease of life, with Ali very much back at the helm. He departed from the ring after his victory over Foreman with a record that now consisted of forty-seven fights, winning forty-five, with two defeats.

Second boxer to regain world heavyweight title

In defeating George Foreman, Muhammad Ali did not just upset the odds against a man who looked unbeatable, he also became the second man in the history of the sport to regain the world heavyweight title. This was really something, and added to the already impressive legacy that Ali had built over the years. Floyd Patterson was the first boxer to regain the crown. He accomplished this feat when he knocked out Sweden's Ingemar Johansson in round five of a scheduled fifteen on 20 June 1960 at the Polo Grounds, New York.

Rope-a-dope

Muhammad Ali used what seemed to be suicidal tactics during his world title challenge to George Foreman. Ali often lay with his back against the ropes while Foreman attacked his body relentlessly with rib-bending punches. Many onlookers wondered what he was doing. This seemed complete madness against a big puncher like Foreman – a ploy that Ali later said was his 'rope-a-dope' plan – a tactic that, let's face it, only Ali would dare to use against a dangerous fighter of Foreman's calibre and get away with it.

Ali bomaye

During the course of the Muhammad Ali–George Foreman world heavyweight title fight, it was more than noticeable that the spectators were firmly on the side of Ali. He was clearly their man, their favourite, their hero. The crowd in attendance wanted the former world heavyweight king to win and rule the division again. Their chants of encouragement of 'Ali bomaye' rang out during the action. When translated into English, the chant means 'Ali, kill him'.

Fight put back

The Muhammad Ali–George Foreman world heavyweight title fight was originally due to take place on 25 September 1974 but was put back to 30 October that year. This was due to the fact that Foreman sustained a bad cut above his right eye when sparring. The wound required eleven stitches, making it impossible for Foreman to defend the championship on the original date.

Chapter 18

Foreman Returns to the Ring

Zach Clayton

The referee of the Muhammad Ali–George Foreman title bout was Zach Clayton, an official who had secured his own place in the pages of boxing history on 5 June 1952. On that date, Clayton refereed the NBA world heavyweight title bout, which saw Jersey Joe Walcott retain the crown over challenger and former champion Ezzard Charles by a fifteen-round points decision. Clayton thus became the first African-American to referee a world heavyweight title contest. The venue for the Walcott–Charles contest was the Municipal Stadium, Philadelphia, Pennsylvania.

A tribute record

It was only a matter of time before it happened: a tribute record to Muhammad Ali. And why not? In 1974, Johnny Wakelin & The Kinshasa Band released a new record called 'Black Superman (Muhammad Ali)'. This was quite appropriate when considering what Ali had achieved to date in his boxing career. The recording was a tribute to the reigning world heavyweight champion and it proved to be very successful both in the UK and the USA.

Ringside for Joe Bugner

On 3 December 1974, Joe Bugner stopped Argentine Alberto Lovell in round two of ten at the Royal Albert Hall, Kensington. It was not a good watch. It was a fight in which Bugner was not able to produce his best against an awkward opponent. Sometimes these things happen in boxing. The styles just do not gel. At ringside, reigning world heavyweight champion Muhammad Ali was a keen observer of the bout since Bugner was a potential challenger for his crown. When the contest was over, Ali took off his shirt and squared up to Bugner, which the spectators enjoyed, perhaps even more so than the actual fight they had come to see.

An audience with Muhammad Ali

On 27 December 1974, the two-time world heavyweight champion appeared on the TV show *An Audience with Muhammad Ali*, hosted by Dickie Davies. Ali, who was very popular in the UK, faced an audience comprising: Reg Gutteridge (boxing journalist), Beryl Cameron-Gibbons (boxing promoter), Henry Cooper (former British, European and Commonwealth heavyweight champion), Len Harvey (former British and Commonwealth middleweight champion, former British and Commonwealth light-heavyweight champion and former British and Commonwealth heavyweight champion), Colin Hart (boxing journalist), Julie Welch (journalist), Frank McGhee (journalist), Alan Hubbard (journalist), Ken Jones (journalist), John Alderton (actor), Ed Stewart (radio broadcaster and TV presenter), Terry Mancini (footballer), Billy Knight (boxer), and Neil Durden-Smith (radio and TV sports presenter). Ali pulled no punches when answering the many questions put to him by the audience in a light-hearted and very comical and entertaining way.

George Foreman reigns again

The defeat to Muhammad Ali on 30 October 1974 was not the end of the George Foreman story as far as world titles were concerned. Anyone who thought that Foreman had had his time in the spotlight and his days of glory were over were very wrong, He was destined to take his own path towards making his own boxing history. It appeared that the thought of Foreman ever becoming a world champion in the division again was laughable to many; he was yesterday's news – an old fighter attempting to recapture past glories of yesteryear, not accepting that his time was over.

Muhammad Ali: The Man Who Changed Boxing

Foreman's first attempt to regain the titles took place on 19 April 1991 against the reigning WBC, WBA and IBF champion Evander Holyfield in New Jersey at the Convention Center in Atlantic City. Holyfield turned back Foreman's challenge when he retained the titles with a twelve-round points decision. The vacant WBO belt was on the line when Foreman stepped up once more in his bid to become a world champion, on 7 June 1993. In the opposite corner was Tommy Morrison, who outscored Foreman over twelve rounds to take the crown, the venue being the Thomas & Mack Center, Las Vegas, Nevada. It seemed that this was the end of the line for Foreman – but it wasn't. Surprisingly, another opportunity presented itself.

On 5 November 1994, at the MGM Grand Garden Arena, Las Vegas, Foreman was given a crack at the WBA and IBF heavyweight king, Michael Moorer. This looked like being another defeat for Foreman. He would take a beating from Moorer and this would finally convince him that his time was over. Well, Foreman was made of stern stuff and took great delight in proving the doubters wrong. The former champion went against the script and regained the world titles by knocking out Moorer in round ten of a scheduled twelve. The man was now back on top of the hill, a champion once more. In so doing, at the age of 45 years, 9 months and 26 days, Foreman became at that time the oldest man to win a world heavyweight championship. It is often said that age is just a number. Foreman, to some extent, proved that theory could be true, and thus gave inspiration to many of similar age.

The longest period of time

When George Foreman defeated Michael Moorer to win the WBA and IBF world heavyweight titles he created yet another record. He clocked up the longest time between losing a world championship and then regaining it in the ring: twenty years and six days.

Amazing to think

George Foreman made his professional debut on 23 June 1969 at Madison Square Garden, New York. His opponent, Don Waldhelm, was stopped in the third stanza of a scheduled six. It is amazing to think that at the time of the contest, Michael Moorer, the man who lost his WBA and IBF world heavyweight titles to Foreman, was just 1 year, 7 months and 11 days old.

Schulz gives Foreman a close fight

George Foreman was later stripped of the WBA version of the championship for his refusal to face the organisation's number-one contender, Tony Tucker. Foreman made the first defence of the IBF portion of the title against Germany's Axel Schulz at the MGM Grand, Las Vegas, on 22 April 1995 – a contest that also included the vacant WBU title. It looked a comfortable fight for Foreman, one he was expected to win. Schulz had comprised a record of twenty-three fights, winning twenty-one, drawing one and losing one. He was good but hardly considered special. That being said, Schulz surprised and gave the champion a tough and close fight. It was a situation where a number of observers felt the German challenger was unlucky not to get the nod and leave the ring as the new champion. A return was ordered by the IBF but Foreman did not accept, and thus had the crown taken from him by the organisation.

George Foreman's last professional contest

After losing his world heavyweight title to Muhammad Ali, George Foreman took part in another forty fights, winning thirty-six and losing four. The respective fights saw him win the WBA, IBF, WBU and IBA versions of the world championship. On 22 November 1997, Foreman took part in his last contest when he lost a twelve-round points decision to Shannon Briggs. The venue for the Foreman–Briggs contest was the Taj Majal hotel and casino, Atlantic City, New Jersey. At the time of the bout, Foreman was 48 years, 10 months and 12 days old. The decision of Foreman not to put on the gloves and compete again was a wise one. He had more than contributed to the sport, both in the amateur and paid code.

During his career, George Foreman participated in eighty-one professional bouts, of which he won seventy-six and lost five.

No threat

Muhammad Ali's world heavyweight title reign did not realistically look to be under threat when he faced challenger Chuck Wepner on 24 March 1975 at the Richfield Coliseum, Ohio. It was considered to be an easy night for the defending champion, merely a routine outing to keep him active until a bigger fight could be made. After his demanding battle against George Foreman in his last bout, Ali more than deserved a less taxing engagement. The challenger was a decent enough boxer but he was nowhere near the level of the champion he was facing. Ali had fought better opponents and defeated them, so it had to be asked, what did Wepner have in his armoury to trouble the king of the division? The obvious answer was very little, except of course courage, which he had in abundance. However, this was boxing and no one should ever be sold short or written off without a hope when competing in the ring.

Heavyweights have a habit of turning the form book upside down. This was Wepner's big chance and truthfully, he had nothing to lose, since few if any gave him any real chance of victory, and this made him a dangerous man. Wepner entered the roped arena with a slate of forty-two contests, winning thirty-one and losing nine, with two drawn. He had it all to play for.

Prior to his meeting with Ali, Wepner had defeated Terry Hinke on 3 September 1974 at Salt Palace, Salt Lake City in Utah, in the eleventh stanza of twelve. The fight was billed as the American heavyweight title. The challenger made the most of his world title chance, putting in a spirited performance against Ali. A surprise took place in round nine, when the champion was floored by Wepner. This was the first time that Ali had been put on the deck when defending his title. This put renewed energy into the contest, which looked like going in just one direction – in Ali's favour. The champion was not seriously hurt; the only injury he suffered was one to his dignity. Ali later showed his remarkable skills and retained his crown when he stopped Wepner in round fifteen. The challenger could leave the ring with his head held high. He may have lost but he left the ring having gained the full respect of the fans in attendance.

Ali's record now stood at forty-six wins, with two defeats.

Chapter 19

Bugner Challenges Ali for the World Heavyweight Title

Second tallest

Chuck Wepner may not have upset the odds by winning the championship but at the reported height of 6 feet 5 inches, he became the second tallest fighter to box Muhammad Ali in a world heavyweight title bout.

Inspired

Reportedly, the Muhammad Ali–Chuck Wepner world heavyweight title contest inspired actor Sylvester Stallone to write the script for the film *Rocky*, which proved to be a massive box-office success.

Chuck Wepner's last professional contest

After his failure to capture the world heavyweight title from Muhammad Ali, Chuck Wepner went on to fight a further nine times, winning five of his bouts and losing four. Wepner, who was nicknamed 'The Bayonne Bleeder', had his last contest on 26 September 1978. On this date he lost a twelve-round points decision to Scott Frank, which saw him say goodbye to his USA New Jersey State heavyweight title. The venue for the Wepner–Frank bout was Ice World, Totowa, New Jersey.

During his career, Chuck Wepner participated in fifty-two professional bouts, winning thirty-six, losing fourteen and drawing two.

First man to stop Ron Lyle

Ron Lyle was not a soft touch, not a fighter to be taken lightly by any opponent he met in the ring. On 16 May 1975, he showed this to be true when challenging Muhammad Ali for the world heavyweight crown. At the Convention Center, Las Vegas, Ali – with a record of forty-eight fights with two defeats – was making the second defence of the championship in his second reign as title holder. Lyle had a slate of thirty-three bouts, with two defeats and one draw. In his last venture into the ring, on 11 February 1975, Lyle had lost a ten-round points decision to Jimmy Young. The contest took place at the Honolulu International Center, Hawaii.

Lyle may have lost to Young but this did not make him any less dangerous. The man was a solid and serious contender who knew a win over Ali would more than make up for his loss to Young and ensure his future in a big way. Lyle was not going to let this golden opportunity pass; he was all in, with victory on his mind. Ali no longer carried the undefeated tag with his name, which meant that a win for him was not an impossibility. Before their date in the ring, both fighters had put in the hours to their training, leaving no stone unturned in their preparation for the fight.

Their fitness showed on the night, with Ali retaining his crown. The champion had to fight hard to win, and win he did in fine style when stopping Lyle in round eleven of fifteen. Not only did Ali retain the title, he also became the first man in the professional ranks to stop Lyle inside the scheduled distance, and that took some doing.

Ron Lyle's last professional contest

Ron Lyle resumed his career after losing in his world title bid to Muhammad Ali, taking to the ring a further seventeen times, winning thirteen and losing on four occasions. Lyle took part in his last contest on 18 August 1995, stopping Dave Slaughter in round two in a bout scheduled for ten. The venue for the Lyle–Slaughter bout was the Regency Hotel, Denver, Colorado.

During his career, Ron Lyle participated in fifty-one professional bouts, winning forty-three, losing seven and drawing one.

Joe Bugner goes the distance

On 30 June 1975, Muhammad Ali made the third defence of his world heavyweight title in his second reign as champion against challenger Joe Bugner. The two were no strangers to each other; Ali had previously outpointed Bugner over twelve rounds on 14 February 1973. Bugner was now more experienced since their first meeting, having indulged in a further nine bouts. Ali, however, once again defeated Bugner when he outpointed him over fifteen rounds at the Merdeka Stadium in Kuala Lumpur.

Ali entered the bout with a record of forty-nine contests, winning forty-seven, with two defeats. Bugner had a slate of fifty-eight bouts, winning fifty-one, with six defeats and one drawn. Bugner, in his last bout, had defended his European crown on 28 February 1975 against challenger Dante Cane by a stoppage in round five of fifteen at the Palazzetto dello Sport, Bologna, Italy. Many Britons hoped that Bugner might be the man to bring the title back to the UK and that he might be in the right place at the right time, but it was not to be. It soon became crystal clear that it was not the right time nor indeed the right place. It really wasn't Bugner's night at all. Ali knew too much for the Briton; he was able to outbox him without too much difficulty. While Bugner may have lost on this occasion, he achieved the distinction of becoming the first British challenger since Welshman Tommy Farr to go the full distance of fifteen rounds in a world heavyweight title challenge.

Tommy Farr's brave challenge

Tommy Farr, like Joe Bugner, faced a great champion in his bid for the world heavyweight title. The fighter holding the crown was Joe Louis. The pair met on 30 August 1937. Farr lost but in defeat, he gained a great deal of respect for his performance against Louis on the night. Boxing purists were of the view prior to the bout that Farr would be lucky to last the distance let alone win the fight. Farr would be destroyed easily by the champion, who was considered to be the perfect fighting machine, a champion who had no equals in the division. Those who doubted the challenger's resolve were made to eat their words, big time.

Farr may have been defeated but in so doing, showed his fighting heart to push the champion all the way through the fifteen-round bout. At no time did Farr look for the easy way out of a tough and punishing contest. The bout for the Louis–Farr contest took place in the USA at the Yankee Stadium, Bronx, New York.

First world heavyweight title contest in Malaysia

The Muhammad Ali–Joe Bugner meeting did not provide thrilling, on-the-edge-of-the-seat action for the fans. It was far from being an epic affair. Many boxing followers expected more from the fight and they had every right to do so. Despite the fight's shortcomings, it was a history maker to some degree, since the Ali–Bugner bout was the first world heavyweight title contest to be staged in Malaysia.

Tallest British challenger

Joe Bugner may have not been the one to bring the championship back to the UK but he became the tallest British boxer to challenge Muhammad Ali for the world heavyweight title, at the reported height of 6 feet 4 inches.

Joe Bugner's last professional contest

Joe Bugner continued to box on after losing to Muhammad Ali in his world heavyweight title challenge, entering the ring on a further twenty-four occasions, of which he won eighteen bouts and lost six. During that period, Bugner won the Australian and Pan Asian Boxing Association heavyweight titles; he also picked up the lightly regarded WBF world heavyweight crown. He eventually called time on his career and thus participated in his last contest on 13 June 1999 against opponent Levi Billups, who was disqualified in round nine in a bout scheduled for ten. The venue for the Bugner–Billlups bout was the Jupiters Hotel and Casino, Broadbeach, Queensland, Australia.

Bugner Challenges Ali for the World Heavyweight Title

During his career, Joe Bugner participated in eighty-three professional bouts, winning sixty-nine, losing thirteen and drawing one.

Only two

It is interesting to note that only two European boxers met Muhammad Ali twice in the professional ring during their careers. Both were British fighters, in the shape of Henry Cooper and Joe Bugner.

Chapter 20

Ali and Frazier Meet for a Third Time

The Thriller in Manilla

On 1 October 1975, Muhammad Ali made the fourth defence in his second reign as world heavyweight champion when he met old rival and former title holder Joe Frazier. Ali had now put together a record of fifty fights, with two defeats. Challenger Frazier was coming into the battle with a resume of thirty-four bouts and two defeats. This was the third meeting between the two fighters, with the score standing at one win each.

This looked to be a promising match but no one could have envisaged what was to come. The two proud boxers really put it on the line during the exciting contest. They gave their all and pushed each other to the very limit of their abilities. This was boxing at its best; this was boxing at its most brutal. The two men's bodies must have been screaming for them to quit during the ardent battle. The word 'quit' was not one that either man recognised. It did not figure in their vocabulary. Their sheer fighting pride drove them on through the blood and pain. It is often said that champions need to have heart as well as skill to win. Well, both Ali and Frazier had a great deal of heart and skill. Their courage and durability was admirable and would be well remembered in the years to come. The mists of time would not and should not erase this fight from the minds of those who keenly follow the sport.

The end came in round fourteen of a scheduled fifteen, when Frazier's corner retired him from the contest. Yet in such a contest, a defeat was not a disgrace. Frazier had contributed to a fight of magnificent intensity – a fight that would be talked about for a long time. The challenger had dug down deep when it seemed there was nothing left to give. So too had Ali, who fought on, draining every inch of strength from his weary body. The fight was dubbed the 'Thriller in Manila', and it was indeed a thriller. It really was one helluva fight.

Don King

American Don King was the promoter of the Muhammad Ali–Joe Frazier world heavyweight title bout, which took place in the Philippines. King, who was born on 20 August 1931 in Cleveland, Ohio, had during his career in boxing promoted a number of a high-profile fights previous to the Ali–Frazier epic. For a period in boxing, King was the man – he had a big say in the boxing world and a really big say in the heavyweight division. He brought the heavy hitters together in marque fights. King, to his credit, had also promoted the historic Muhammad Ali–George Foreman world heavyweight title bout on 30 October 1974, which saw Ali regain the heavyweight crown.

First world heavyweight championship to be held in the Philippines

The contest between Muhammad Ali and Joe Frazier was held at the Araneta Coliseum, Barangay Cubao, Quezon City, Metro Manila in the Philippines. This was a special event since it was the first time that a world heavyweight title contest had taken place in the Philippines – and what a first it was for the division, and for the country.

Joe Frazier comeback

After his failed attempt to regain the world heavyweight championship from Muhammad Ali, Joe Frazier had one more contest, on 15 June 1976, against George Foreman in a challenge for the NABF heavyweight title. The venue was the Nassau Coliseum, Uniondale, New York. Frazier was stopped in round five of a scheduled twelve. He later retired from the sport. It looked as if that was it from Frazier. There was nowhere else for him to go with regards to actual combat in the ring. He could do no more. On 3 December 1981, there was an air of surprise when Frazier made a comeback to boxing. He put the gloves back on and participated in a contest that took place at the International Amphitheatre, Chicago, Illinois. The opponent facing Frazier was Floyd Cummings, who came into the ring with a record consisting of sixteen bouts, winning fifteen and losing one.

The defeat on Cummings's resume came at the hands of Renaldo Snipes on 8 March 1981, when losing a ten-round points decision.

The Frazier–Cummings bout went the full ten rounds, resulting in a draw. This must have been very disappointing for Frazier, who would have wanted to have made a statement with an impressive performance against Cummings. Clearly, this was not the Frazier of old; the fire that once drove the man was now diminished. At his peak, Cummings would not have lasted the distance with the former world heavyweight champion, let alone attain a draw. The bitter truth that fighters on the comeback trail eventually have to confront is that their time has passed and their best days are behind them. This proved to be Frazier's last contest. After the Frazier fight, Cummings had a further five bouts, all of which he lost.

During his career, Joe Frazier participated in thirty-seven professional bouts, of which he won thirty-two and lost four, with one draw.

First challenger from Belgium

Muhammad Ali made the fifth defence in his second reign of his world heavyweight championship on 20 February 1976, against Belgium's Jean-Pierre Coopman. The challenger climbed between the ropes with a record of twenty-seven fights, with twenty-four wins and three defeats. Ali had now built up a resume of fifty-one bouts, with two defeats.

The venue for the bout was the Roberto Clemente Coliseum, San Juan, Puerto Rico. Looking at the contest realistically, the challenger had very little chance of defeating Ali to become the new champion. Ali was leagues above Coopman and in the past had beaten opponents who were at a much higher level. There was nothing at all in the Belgian's resume that might suggest he would pose a threat of any kind to the title holder. The fight looked to be a no-risk outing for Ali. There was the chance that he would slip one day in the future and suffer another defeat but that was not going to be today, not against Coopman. Ali remained king of the world when the bout, scheduled for fifteen rounds, ended in the fifth, whereupon Ali won by a knockout. The champion was hardly troubled by anything Coopman threw at him during the contest; he really had it all his own way. It is often said that the lion is the king of the jungle. Well, that may or may not be true. Coopman was nicknamed the 'Lion of Flanders', but this lion was far from being the king of the ring: he failed to roar even once during the encounter.

Coopman may not have been able to take the title back home but he had, at least, the honour of becoming the first Belgian in the long history of the sport to challenge for the heavyweight championship of the world. So that is something to Coopman's credit.

Jean-Pierre Coopman's last professional contest

The defeat by Muhammad Ali in his world heavyweight title bid put paid to any ideas Jean-Pierre Coopman may have had of being a world-class fighter let alone a future world title holder. However, he continued with his profession, taking part in a further twenty-six fights, winning twelve and losing twelve, with two draws. He also won the European heavyweight crown. Coopman had his last contest on 5 April 1999, against Freddy De Kerpel, which resulted in a draw over six rounds. The venue for the Coopman–De Kerpel bout was Ghent, in the province of Oost-Vlaanderen, Belgium.

During his career, Jean-Pierre Coopman participated in fifty-four professional bouts, of which he won thirty-six, losing sixteen, with two drawn.

A tricky opponent

Muhammad Ali was in action once again on 30 April 1976, at the Capital Center, Landover, Maryland. Ali was making the sixth defence of his world heavyweight crown in his second reign. Ali's record now stood at fifty-two fights, winning fifty, with two defeats. On this occasion, the challenger facing Ali was Jimmy Young, who had accumulated during his career twenty-three bouts, winning seventeen, losing four and drawing two.

In his last outing, which had taken place on 20 February 1976, Young outpointed José Roman over ten rounds at the Roberto Clemente Coliseum, San Juan, Puerto Rico. Young was considered a good fighter but not one who was likely to concern Ali in any way whatsoever. Those who knew the fight game felt that he was a challenger who would be clearly beaten by the champion, either inside the distance or on points. After his battle with the likes of Joe Frazier, this contest by comparison looked like being an easy ride, a tame affair, one perhaps that Ali would be able to win in his stride without working up too much of a sweat. He just had to turn up, get the job done and go home. It really could not be easier. Well, that was the expert view before the bout. On the night, Young surprised many by proving to be a very tricky and frustrating opponent for the champion. Ali had to work hard to retain his title on points after fifteen rounds. The fight, to say the least, provided very little in the way of excitement value. A number of critics who were not impressed by Ali's performance considered it below par.

Ali at his heaviest

In his world heavyweight title defence against Jimmy Young, Muhammad Ali came into the bout at a reported weight of 230lb. This was the heaviest Ali had ever been in a world title contest.

Second man to defeat George Foreman

In his fourth fight after losing to Muhammad Ali, Jimmy Young confirmed that he was a difficult opponent for anyone in the division to handle. On 17 March 1977, he entered the ring to face former world heavyweight king George Foreman at the Roberto Clemente Coliseum, San Juan, Puerto Rico. Young had now participated in twenty-seven bouts, winning twenty, losing five and drawing two. At the time, Foreman, with a resume of forty-six bouts with one defeat, was a fearsome puncher looking to get back into the ring with Ali. When examining the stats of both fighters' records it looked as if Foreman would punch his way to victory. Young ended such plans when he outpointed Foreman over twelve rounds. Young became just the second man to beat Foreman in the professional ranks. Soon after his defeat by Young, Foreman retired from boxing. This looked like the end of Foreman – but he would return.

Chapter 21

Ali Defeats another Briton

Frequent UK visitor

British fight fans were more than aware of the ring capabilities of Jimmy Young. The American fought on four occasions in the UK. Young showed his skill set in his first bout in Britain, whereupon he boxed an eight-round draw with Billy Aird on 22 October 1973. The bout took place at the Grosvenor House Sporting Club, Mayfair, London. Then, in 1974, he stopped future British, European and Commonwealth heavyweight king Richard Dunn in round eight of ten. The contest took place on 18 February at the World Sporting Club, Mayfair. Young later outpointed Les Stevens over the duration of ten rounds on 22 April, the venue being the Grosvenor House, Mayfair. The British and Commonwealth heavyweight king John L. Gardner was then outpointed over ten rounds by the American visitor on 4 December 1979 at the Empire Pool, Wembley.

Jimmy Young's last professional contest

After he failed in his world heavyweight title challenge against Muhammad Ali, Jimmy Young fought on and participated in a further thirty-three bouts, of which he won eighteen, lost thirteen, drew one, with one no contest. Young had his last professional fight on 22 September 1990 at the Mississippi Coast Coliseum, Biloxi, California, where he went out on a winning note, stopping his opponent Carl Porter in round two of a bout scheduled for six. During his career, Jimmy Young had participated in fifty-seven professional bouts, winning thirty-five, losing eighteen and drawing three, with one no contest.

Dunn the first

Muhammad Ali made the seventh defence of his world heavyweight title in his second reign as champion on 24 May 1976 at the Olympiahalle, Munich, Germany. His opponent was Britain's Richard Dunn. Dunn was the fourth British boxer to challenge Ali for the crown after the futile attempts of Henry Cooper in 1966, Brian London, also in 1966, and Joe Bugner in 1975. Dunn had the distinction of being the first challenger from the UK with the southpaw stance to challenge for the title. At the time, Dunn was the reigning British, European and Commonwealth heavyweight king. The Briton entered the contest with a professional record of forty-two bouts, winning thirty-three, with nine defeats.

In his previous bout before stepping in with Ali, Dunn had won the vacant European heavyweight title, on 6 April 1976, when stopping Germany's Bernd August in the third stanza of fifteen. The bout took place at the Royal Albert Hall, Kensington, London. Dunn was last defeated on 22 May 1974, when he was knocked out in round four of eight by Spain's former two-time European heavyweight title holder José Manuel Urtain. The venue for the Dunn–Urtain bout was the Palacio de los Deportes, Madrid, Spain. At that moment in time, any thoughts of Dunn ever fighting for a world heavyweight title would have been considered nothing more than a dream. Well, it is often said that dreams can come true. In Dunn's case, the dream did materialise. After the setback in Spain against Urtain, Dunn put together seven wins, which put him in the position of challenging for the title. Ali had an impressive record of fifty-three contests, with just two defeats. The pundits did not give Dunn any chance of victory against Ali – a view that even the casual fans of the sport agreed with. It really was difficult to see how he could find a way to defeat Ali. The Briton had not fought anyone near the class of Ali during the course of his entire career. Therefore, it was not a matter of if he would get beaten, but in which round he would get beaten.

Dunn may have been at a disadvantage with regard to his ring skills when up against one of the greats in the sport. Yet falling short against a man like Ali was no disgrace. Higher rated fighters than Dunn had not been able to get the better of him in the past. During the contest, Dunn showed both courage and determination in his bid to dislodge the crown from Ali. The Briton gave everything he had but it was not enough; the title holder was way above his challenger with his skill set.

Ali Defeats another Briton

The British fighter was outclassed and it showed from the opening bell. The champion brought the proceedings to a close when he stopped Dunn in round five of a scheduled fifteen to retain his crown.

Dunn the second

Richard Dunn was only the second boxer with the southpaw stance to win the British heavyweight title. Dunn duly won the championship, and the Commonwealth crown when he defeated Danny McAlinden on 4 November 1975 by a knockout in two rounds in a contest scheduled for fifteen. The Dunn–McAlinden bout took place at the Empire Pool, Wembley.

Two southpaws

In defeating Richard Dunn, Muhammad Ali became the first world heavyweight champion to defend his crown against two boxers who had fought in the southpaw stance. The first of these was Karl Mildenberger, on 10 September 1966, when Ali retained the title by stopping his challenger in round twelve of fifteen. Both encounters with southpaws, Mildenberger and Dunn, took place in Germany.

Last stoppage win by Ali

When Richard Dunn was stopped by Muhammad Ali in round five of fifteen during his world title challenge he became the last fighter to be halted inside the scheduled distance by the American. Dunn was also the last boxer to be floored by him during a contest. Dunn was put on the canvas five times during the course of the bout.

Richard Dunn's last professional contest

After his failed bid to win the world heavyweight crown from Muhammad Ali, Richard Dunn took part in two more bouts. On

12 October 1976, he lost his British, Commonwealth and European titles to Joe Bugner when knocked out in the first of a scheduled fifteen-round contest. The venue for the fight was the Empire Pool, Wembley. In his next outing, on 10 September 1977, Dunn travelled to South Africa to meet Kallie Knoetze at the Ellis Park Tennis Stadium, Johannesburg. The bout was set for the duration of ten rounds but only lasted until the fifth, whereupon Dunn was knocked out by his opponent. The British fighter realised that his career was now over and he later retired from the sport. Dunn thus became the only boxer to lose every one of his fights after meeting Ali in a world heavyweight title contest.

During his professional career, Richard Dunn participated in forty-five fights, winning thirty-three and losing twelve.

Boxer v wrestler

On 26 June 1976, Muhammad Ali met Antonio Inoki, a Japanese professional wrestler. The fight provided fans with a boxer v wrestler contest – a mixture of the two sports – and was billed as 'The War of The Worlds'. The spectacle of such a meeting may have appeared to be an exciting event between two sporting giants meeting inside the ring. An action-packed event looked assured – one to look forward to, a fascinating encounter. However, the fifteen-round exhibition bout, which took place at the Nippon Budokan in Tokyo, ended in a draw. The match between the two failed to live up to expectations, with few, if any, exciting moments during their meeting.

Ali–Norton 3

Muhammad Ali made the eighth defence of the world heavyweight championship in his second reign as title holder on 28 September 1976, when he met his old foe Ken Norton for the third time in the paid ranks. Ali now had a resume of fifty-four fights, with just two defeats. Norton's record now read forty fights, with thirty-seven wins and three defeats. This would be the decider for the pair, with the score standing at one win each.

Ali Defeats another Briton

The contest took place at the Yankee Stadium, Bronx, New York. While one had to favour Ali to get the better of Norton, it was not a confident prediction. It was no secret that Norton had a style that presented Ali with all kinds of problems. He was a nightmare for the champion in every sense of the word. The two fighters knew each other inside out. Looking at the bout realistically, it would not have been a massive surprise had Norton won the title from the champion. After a bruising battle, Ali prevailed on points after fifteen rounds to retain his title. It was not an easy victory for Ali – far from it. The champion had to fight hard to ensure he left the ring with the crown. The two did not meet again in the ring, which deep down may well have pleased Ali greatly.

Ken Norton acquires the WBC world heavyweight title

Ken Norton went on to acquire world championship status when the WBC stripped Leon Spinks of the title when he signed to fight Muhammad Ali in a return contest rather than Norton, who was their number-one contender. Norton was thus proclaimed champion by the WBC, without even throwing a punch. The new title holder would have much preferred to have won the crown the traditional way inside the ring to obtain the desired honour. Norton had previously outpointed Jimmy Young over fifteen rounds on 5 November 1977 in an eliminator for the WBC title. The contest took place at Caesars Palace Sports Pavilion, Las Vegas, Nevada.

Norton's reign did not last too long since he lost the crown in his first defence, against Larry Holmes on 9 June 1978, by a fifteen-round points decision. The venue was Caesars Palace Sports Pavilion, Las Vegas, Nevada. Norton's first crack at the championship had taken place in El Poliedro, Caracas, Venezuela, on 26 March 1974, against the then holder, George Foreman. This was for the undisputed title. He was stopped in the second session of a fifteen-round contest. Consequently, Norton has the unusual distinction of being a world champion without ever having won a title fight.

Ken Norton's last professional contest

After being defeated by Muhammad Ali in his world heavyweight title challenge, Ken Norton took part in a further nine fights, winning five, losing three and drawing one. He was able to obtain the WBC version of the world crown later down the line. On 11 May 1981, Norton bowed out of boxing at the Madison Square Garden, New York, in a fight against hard-hitting opponent Gerry Cooney, who stopped him in the opening round of a scheduled ten. The defeat indicated that it was time for Norton to walk away from the sport. His best was now well behind him and it was sensible to say goodbye.

Ken Norton participated in fifty professional bouts during his career, winning forty-two and losing seven, with one drawn.

Chapter 22

Ali Shocked by Spinks

First from Uruguay

Muhammad Ali's challenger, Alfredo Evangelista, did not have a hope of taking the world heavyweight title away from him. On the European circuit, Evangelista was a good fighter, but there are good fighters and great fighters, and Ali was a great fighter. That was the difference between the two. There was no getting away from the fact that Ali was light years ahead of his latest challenger. Evangelista came to do battle with a resume of sixteen fights, having won fourteen and lost one, with one drawn. Ali, who was making the ninth defence of his championship in his second title reign, entered the contest with a record of fifty-five fights, with just two defeats. The two defeats, of course, came at the hands of Joe Frazier and Ken Norton, and Evangelista was no Frazier, nor a Norton. When first announced, the fight did not exactly whet the appetite of boxing fans. It seemed that Ali would waltz his way to victory without exerting himself too much, notching up yet another successful title defence.

The championship fight took place on 16 May 1977. The venue for the bout was the Capital Center, Landover, Maryland. Ali, as expected, retained his crown, with a fifteen-round points win over his challenger. To his credit, Evangelista gave a spirited performance against the champion. He chased Ali from round one, throwing punch after punch. Therefore, no one can doubt his commitment during the fight. This was his big chance and he was making the most of the opportunity. The fight was not one that could be called exciting in any way; there was no real drama. Evangelista, whilst a Spanish resident, was in fact born in Uruguay and as such became the first boxer from that country to challenge for the world heavyweight championship.

No luck for Evangelista

After being defeated by Muhammad Ali, Alfredo Evangelista had a further sixty-two bouts, winning forty-eight and losing eleven, with three drawn. During that time, he also won the European crown on two separate occasions, as well as securing a second opportunity to win a version of the world heavyweight crown. This took place on 10 November 1978. The defending title holder in the opposite corner was WBC king, Larry Holmes. The venue for the bout was the Caesars Palace Sports Pavilion, Las Vegas. Evangelista had not been given any chance of pulling off a victory when he faced Muhammad Ali, but he surprised many in his performance by lasting the full fifteen rounds. Once again, he was the underdog against Holmes. The question was, could he produce something special to upset the odds? The answer was a resounding no. The title remained in the USA when Holmes retained the crown by way of a knockout in the seventh stanza in a bout that was scheduled for fifteen rounds.

Alfredo Evangelista's last professional contest

Alfredo Evangelista took part in his last contest on 15 April 1988 against opponent Arthur Wright, winning by a knockout in round two of a scheduled ten. The venue for the Evangelista–Wright bout was the Comunidad de Madrid, Spain.

During his professional career, Alfredo Evangelista participated in seventy-nine fights, winning sixty-two and losing thirteen, with four drawn.

The Greatest

In 1977, Muhammad Ali played himself in a biographical film titled *The Greatest*. This was an interesting movie, which featured well-known film actor Ernest Borgnine as Angelo Dundee. The rest of the cast included Roger E. Mosley as Sonny Liston, John Marley as Dr Ferdie Pacheco, with Drew Bundini Brown (Ali's assistant trainer and cornerman) playing himself. The production proved to be an entertaining watch for the many fans of Ali. It is always a challenge for someone to play himself in a film, but Ali pulled it off in style.

Ali Shocked by Spinks

A dangerous opponent

On 29 September 1977, Muhammad Ali entered the ring at Madison Square Garden, New York, to defend his world heavyweight crown for the tenth time in his second reign, against the hard-punching Earnie Shavers. Ali emerged successful, with a points victory over fifteen rounds to retain his title. Prior to meeting Ali, Shavers had participated in sixty bouts, winning fifty-four and losing five, with one drawn. Shavers was known for his punching power, having won fifty-two of his bouts inside the scheduled distance. He was always a threat to anyone with whom he shared the ring. If he found the target with his blows, his opponent was in big trouble – trouble with a capital T. Shavers did not come to play the victim when he fought, he came to fight and fight hard, putting everything on the line. Every punch he threw, he threw with bad intentions; there was no softly, softly approach with his brand of boxing. He was always looking to take out an opponent early and never had any intention of going the distance if he could help it.

In his previous contest before the dual with Ali, on 16 April 1977, Shavers had fought against Howard Smith at the Aladdin Theatre, Las Vegas, when he left the ring victorious after winning by a knockout in round two of ten. He had last tasted defeat on 13 September 1975, when coming up against another big puncher in the shape of Ron Lyle, at the Denver Coliseum, Colorado. The fight was set for the duration of twelve rounds but the power of the two men made it obvious that this was not going the full distance. It came to a close when Shavers was knocked out in round six. Shavers regrouped after the setback and won his next five on the bounce. He was now more than ready to rumble and was confident that he would be able to nail Ali and put him away and take the title.

Ali had previously participated in fifty-six bouts, losing on just two occasions. True to his reputation, Shavers gave the champion a tough time, connecting a number of times with his solid blows, which clearly hurt him. Ali was walking on a minefield with Shavers: one slip, one wrong move and boom, it was all over. Both men needed all the oxygen their bodies could take in. It was a credit to Ali's fitness and durability that he was able to absorb the punches that landed to his head and torso.

The contest concluded with an exciting final round, with both fighters digging down deep in their efforts to win. The fans in attendance were on their feet with the excitement, watching the two warriors trading punch for punch and refusing to give an inch. Spectators could not take their eyes off the action for one moment. The challenger was dangerous right up to the final bell, always looking for the payoff punch, the one that would say goodnight to Ali and see him take the crown home. It was a punishing contest for Ali and Shavers, who had both been hurt during the encounter. Ali had now taken part in fifty-seven fights, winning fifty-five and losing two. The bout against Shavers proved to be the very last time that Ali would a fight at the Garden.

First woman judge

The contest between Muhammad Ali and Earnie Shavers proved to be an historic one for a reason other than the fact that Ali was involved. The history maker in question was Eva Shain, who became the first woman to be a judge at a world heavyweight title fight. This was a major step for women's involvement in boxing.

Earnie Shavers' last professional contest

After being defeated by Muhammad Ali for the world heavyweight crown, Earnie Shavers had a further thirty bouts, winning twenty-two and losing eight. He also had another crack at the world crown.

The second bite of the apple took place on 28 September 1979. Shavers stepped into the ring with the then reigning WBC title holder, Larry Holmes. The venue for the contest was Caesars Palace, Las Vegas. Shavers and Holmes were no strangers to each other; they had previously fought on 25 March 1978, the venue for that meeting also being Caesars Palace. The contest was a WBC world title eliminator. Holmes came through with a win when gaining a twelve-round points decision. In his bid against Holmes for the championship, Shavers pulled out all the stops. He was determined, and being a warrior, gave it his all, but to no avail. His brave challenge came to an end in round eleven of a scheduled fifteen. The referee stopped the bout in favour of the defending title holder after an exciting bout. The hard-fought contest saw Holmes floored for a count in the seventh stanza by Shavers. Holmes survived the scare and battled back to secure the victory.

On 24 November 1995, Brian Yates knocked out Shavers in round two in a contest that was set for ten rounds. This indicated that the former two-time world title challenger's long and distinctive career had come to the end of the road. The venue for the Shavers–Yates bout was the Ho-Chunk Casino, Baraboo, Wisconsin.

During his professional career, Earnie Shavers had participated in ninety-one fights, winning seventy-six and losing fourteen, with one drawn.

Didn't expect that

No one felt that Muhammad Ali would lose his title on 15 February 1978 when he defended his world heavyweight crown against challenger Leon Spinks at the Hilton Hotel, Las Vegas. The challenger was a good fighter but was regarded in professional terms as a mere novice due to his lack of experience at top level. The contest was looked upon as a routine outing for the champion, who was making his eleventh defence in his second title reign. It really appeared as if the chance for Spinks had come too soon and that he would have found it more beneficial having a few more bouts under his belt before going for the title. This looked a reasonable assumption under the circumstances.

The challenger came into the ring with a resume of seven fights, winning six, with one draw. In his last bout, on 18 November 1977, Spinks had outpointed Alfio Rigetti of Italy over ten rounds at the Hilton Hotel, Las Vegas. Now that wasn't a bad win for Spinks, since Rigetti had come to fight with an undefeated record that stood at twenty-seven. Yet it wasn't a victory that indicated Spinks was going to be the next heavyweight title holder. Rigetti was no Ali; he was nowhere near his class. Spinks had not fought anyone of real note, so how could he possibly overcome a man who had dominated the division for so many years? But the sport is unpredictable, as many events had proven over the years. If you were pushed to have a gamble on the outcome, you would surely have put your money on Ali retaining the title. He was the obvious choice. However, had you indeed placed a bet on an Ali win, you would have been seriously out of pocket. Over the years, Ali had constantly shocked the world by doing the impossible. In this contest, it was the challenger who shocked the world and defeated Ali by a fifteen-round points decision.

While Spinks did well to rise to the massive task in front of him, many wondered if it was the passing of time rather than the skills of the challenger that had defeated Ali. The former champion's record now read fifty-eight bouts, with just three defeats.

Two former Olympic light-heavyweights

When Muhammad Ali defended his title against Leon Spinks, it was the first time that two former Olympic gold medal winners from the light-heavyweight division had fought each other in a world heavyweight title fight.

Wins title in just his eighth professional contest

When Leon Spinks defeated Muhammad Ali, he put his name in the record books by winning the championship in just his eighth professional contest. This was a remarkable achievement by any lengths. No previous boxer in the history of the sport had ever won this crown with so few fights behind him.

Chapter 23

Ali Back on Top of the World

First boxer to regain the world heavyweight title twice

When Leon Spinks defeated Muhammad Ali to capture the world heavyweight title on 15 February 1978, it would be an understatement to say it was a shock. A return between the pair just had to happen. It was crying out to be made. Ali wanted to show that he underperformed the first time around against Spinks, having an off night. Spinks, in turn, wanted to show that he once again had the mastery to defeat Ali, a man still revered by all. The two fighters had a point to prove in this return. It was all adding up to much more than just an interesting meeting between the pair – there was a great deal at stake in this contest. Should Ali lose, there would be no way back for him, that was the simple truth. His days in the ring would be over. A defeat for Spinks, too, would be damaging, but he was at an age where it was more than possible for him to come again. So perhaps the pressure for him wasn't as bad as the one Ali had to bear when preparing for the fight.

The bout took place on 15 September 1978 at the Superdome, New Orleans, Louisiana. This time, Ali was on his game and boxed his way to a fifteen-round points decision. This was a moment of glory for Ali – a history maker. The victory saw him become the first man to regain the title on two occasions. (Only the WBA crown was at stake in this bout since the WBC had stripped Spinks of their version of the title for his failure to defend against Ken Norton.) It appeared that this was Ali's last hurrah for he later announced his retirement from boxing. This looked to be the ideal time for Ali to hang up his gloves, going out on a win with a record of fifty-nine bouts, with just three defeats. This would have been the perfect ending to a magnificent career.

A new record for indoor attendance

The return world heavyweight title fight between Muhammad Ali and Leon Spinks was obviously going to be one that would sell, such was the public interest in the bout. The box-office returns on the night were more than healthy, providing the sport with yet another milestone in that the fight set a new record for the reported highest indoor attendance of spectators to witness a boxing contest, the total being 63,350.

Spinks attempts to become a world heavyweight title holder once again

On 12 June 1981, Leon Spinks secured a contest with reigning WBC world heavyweight title holder Larry Holmes at the Joe Louis Arena, Detroit, Michigan. Spinks, who had lost his WBA title to Muhammad Ali on 15 September 1978, felt he could reign once more at the top of the division. Going into the fight, Holmes was the firm favourite to retain the title, and with good reason. The champion was a class act, who was on splendid form on the night and won with ultimate ease. Holmes stopped Spinks in round three of a scheduled fifteen-round contest. Spinks now looked to be a spent force in the division.

Spinks moves down a weight division

Despite his defeats to Muhammad Ali and Larry Holmes, Leon Spinks was not finished in his bid to hold a world crown once again, if not at heavyweight then in some other division. On 22 March 1986, he dropped to a lower division and challenged Dwight Muhammad Qawi for the WBA cruiserweight title. Qawi was a good champion who was more than ready to take on the challenge that confronted him. Spinks entered the ring determined to take the crown, but despite his determination, he failed in his bid. Qawi was just too good for him. The former world heavyweight king was stopped in round six of a contest set for the duration of fifteen. The title bout took place at the Lawlor Events Center in Reno, Nevada. This fight saw for the first time a situation whereby a former world heavyweight champion moved down to the cruiserweight poundage and hence challenged for a world crown.

Leon Spinks's last professional contest

After losing his WBA world heavyweight title to Muhammad Ali on 15 September 1978, Leon Spinks took part in a further thirty-seven fights, of which he won nineteen, lost sixteen and drew two. Spinks's final appearance in the ring took place on 4 December 1995 against opponent Fred Houpe. The venue for the contest was A Little Bit of Texas, Saint Louis, Missouri. Spinks lost the bout by way of an eight-round points decision. It was clear that the former world heavyweight king had come to the end of the road and his fighting days were well and truly over.

During his professional career, Leon Spinks participated in forty-six bouts, winning twenty-six and losing seventeen, with three drawn.

A surprise for Muhammad Ali

Muhammad Ali, a frequent visitor to the UK, became the subject of the TV show *This is Your Life* in December 1978. The programme, introduced by Eamonn Andrews, looked back on Ali's life and saw a number of guests brought onto the show giving their recollections of the great three-time world heavyweight champion. The guests included: Ali's then wife, Veronica; his parents, Odessa and Cassius Clay Snr, and his brother, Rahman Ali; singer Tom Jones; former WBA world heavyweight title holder Jimmy Ellis; Ali's first amateur opponent, Ronnie O'Keefe; Joe E. Martin, who introduced Ali to boxing; Ali's trainer, Fred Stoner, and his professional trainer, Angelo Dundee; Zbigniew Pietrzykowski, who fought Ali in the Olympic Games final. Also in attendance were: Wilma Rudolph, a sprinter who won three gold medals at the Rome Olympic Games; Drew Bundini Brown, assistant trainer; Howard Bingham, a friend and a renowned photographer; former British, European and Commonwealth heavyweight king Henry Cooper; and former undisputed world heavyweight champion Joe Frazier.

Freedom road

Continuing to prove his versatility outside of the boxing ring, Muhammad Ali portrayed the role of Gideon Jackson, an ex-slave who becomes a US senator in the 1979 mini-series *Freedom Road*. Kris Kristofferson also starred in the production as Abner Lait. The cast included Barbara O. Jones and Ron O'Neal.

First man to stop Ali

On 2 October 1980, Muhammad Ali returned to the ring and attempted to create even more history in boxing when attempting to regain a version of the world heavyweight title for a third time. The return to the square ring proved to be an unwise decision. The odds were against Ali, but the former champion had overcome the odds before, so could he do it again? There is an old saying in boxing that 'they never come back'. Could Ali disprove this and show he still had what it takes to be king of the world? Ali was going up against the reigning WBC king, Larry Holmes, who was undefeated in thirty-five bouts and very much in his prime. Holmes looked to be special, an exceptional champion. While holding just a version of the title, Holmes was considered the top man in the division at the time of the fight.

Holmes was proving to be an active champion, making the eighth defence of the title. He had won the crown from Ken Norton by way of a fifteen-round points decision on 9 June 1978. Earlier in his career, Holmes had once been a sparring partner for Ali, so the fighters knew each other well. The venue for the Holmes–Ali fight was Caesars Palace, Las Vegas. Ali was taking part in his sixtieth contest, having previously won fifty-seven of his bouts and losing three. Ali had not fought since he regained the WBA crown from Leon Spinks on 15 September 1978. Ali retired soon after his victory over Spinks. Many in Vegas go to the city to gamble at the casinos. Some win, some lose. Many of the winners continue to play on after they should have quit. Having just that one more throw of the dice or the last spin of the wheel is always tempting, but it often proves to be a disaster. Ali should not have returned to the ring, he should not have taken that last throw of the dice or the last spin of the wheel. None of us can halt the passing of time; we like to think we can but truthfully, we cannot. Not even great champions can do that. It was obvious that time had caught up with Ali and to be brutally frank, he was past his sell-by date. The expiry date affects everyone, no matter what their profession. The trick is accepting it and coming to terms with it. Holmes not only retained his crown but also became the first fighter in the professional ranks to stop Ali inside the scheduled distance. This was a sad moment for the fans of the former champion. Ali failed to answer the bell for round eleven of a contest set for fifteen. He made a fight of it against Holmes; he was a fighter and was not going to go out easily. However, that night he became another loser in Vegas.

Last man to referee a Muhammad Ali world heavyweight title contest

The third man in the ring for the Larry Holmes–Muhammad Ali WBC heavyweight title fight was Richard Green, who thus became the last man to referee Ali in a world title contest.

Last judges to officiate at a Muhammad Ali world heavyweight title contest

The three judges to officiate at the last world heavyweight title bout involving Muhammad Ali were Duane Ford, Chuck Minker and Richard Steele.

Last man to promote a Muhammad Ali world heavyweight title contest

Don King was the promoter of the Larry Holmes–Muhammad Ali WBC world heavyweight title contest and hence became the last man to promote a world championship that involved Ali.

Chapter 24

The Last Contest

Larry Holmes's last professional contest

After successfully defending the WBC world heavyweight title against Muhammad Ali, Larry Holmes participated in a further thirty-nine fights, winning thirty-three and losing six of the outings. He also became the first holder of the IBF version of the world heavyweight crown. Holmes had his last contest on 27 July 2002, outpointing opponent Eric Esch, also known as 'Butterbean', over ten rounds. The Holmes–Esch bout took place at the Scope Arena, Norfolk, Virginia.

During his career, Larry Holmes participated in seventy-five professional bouts, of which he won sixty-nine and lost six.

Muhammad Ali's last professional contest

It was hoped that the defeat against Larry Holmes would persuade Muhammad Ali to finally hang up his gloves and quit the ring. Sadly, it was not to be. He returned to the ring on 11 December 1981. Many frowned when they heard the news, knowing that this was a terrible mistake. The venue for the contest was the Queen Elizabeth Sports Centre, Nassau in the Bahamas. The fight was tagged 'The Drama in the Bahamas'. The opponent in the opposite corner to Ali was the reigning Commonwealth heavyweight champion, Trevor Berbick, who entered the contest with a resume of twenty-two bouts, winning nineteen and losing two, with one drawn.

Berbick had been defeated by Larry Holmes in a WBC world heavyweight title shot on 11 April 1981, when outpointed over fifteen rounds at Caesars Palace Sports Pavilion, Las Vegas. Ali now had a record of sixty bouts, winning fifty-six and losing four. Berbick, it must be said, was not a bad fighter; he was a handful for most opponents he met and he always came to fight. Even though Ali was past his best, a win on Berbick's resume would not do him any harm. Ali at his peak would surely have given Berbick a boxing lesson and won without question. However, that was in the past. Ali was now very much in the present and was feeling the full weight of time on his shoulders. The realities of life showed just how much the skills of the once great champion had deteriorated over recent years. Despite this, Ali gave a good account of himself during the contest, often scoring with good jabs throughout the bout. The man was a revelation; he was a warrior through and through. He was not going out easy; he was going to make a fight of it until the bitter end, until the final bell had sounded. When the fight concluded, the ten-round points decision went to Berbick. This proved to be Ali's last contest. There would be no coming back from this defeat.

Age difference

At the time of his contest with Trevor Berbick, Muhammad Ali was 39 years, 10 months and 24 days old. This begs the oft-asked question, where did the time go? Berbick was the much younger man, aged 27 years, 4 months and 10 days.

Last man to referee a Muhammad Ali contest

The third man in the ring during the Muhammad Ali–Trevor Berbick contest was Zach Clayton, who became the last referee to be in charge of a professional bout that involved Ali.

Last judges to officiate at a Muhammad Ali contest

Alonzo Butler, Jay Edson and Clyde Gray were the last judges to officiate at a Muhammad Ali contest.

Shocked by the news

For some time after his retirement from boxing, Muhammad Ali had been showing signs of ill health during his public appearances. There was speculation about the cause of his illness. Then, in 1984, it was announced that Ali had been diagnosed with Parkinson's disease. Many were shocked and saddened by this news.

Married life

Muhammad Ali married on four occasions. His wives were:

Sonji Roi	1964–66
Belinda Boyd (Khalilah Ali)	1967–76
Veronica Porsche	1977–86
Yolanda 'Lonnie' Williams	1986 until his death

Only four

Muhammad Ali fought a number of hard-hitting fighters when competing in the professional ranks and in that time was only floored four times. The boxers who scored the knockdowns were Sonny Banks (1962), Henry Cooper (1963), Joe Frazier (1971), and Chuck Wepner (1975). This speaks volumes for the heart and durability that Ali possessed alongside his boxing skills.

Drew Bundini Brown

Drew Bundini Brown, who joined Muhammad Ali's team in 1963 as a cornerman and assistant trainer, passed away on 24 September 1987. Brown, born on 21 March 1928 in Florida, was a colourful character and proved to be an asset to Ali during his time with him.

Madison Square Garden

Muhammad Ali boxed at Madison Square Garden in New York more often than at any other venue during his professional career, the total being eight times, as follows:

The Last Contest

10 February 1962	Sonny Banks	Won, by a four-round stoppage
13 March 1963	Doug Jones	Won, ten-round points decision
22 March 1967	Zora Folley	Won, knockout round seven (Retained world heavyweight title)
7 December 1970	Oscar Bonavena	Won, stoppage in round fifteen
8 March 1971	Joe Frazier	Lost, fifteen-round points decision (Failed to regain world heavyweight crown)
20 September 1972	Floyd Patterson	Won, retired round seven (Retained NABF heavyweight title)
28 January 1974	Joe Frazier	Won, twelve-round points decision (Retained NABF heavyweight title)
29 September 1977	Earnie Shavers	Won, fifteen-round points decision) (Retained world heavyweight title)

Chapter 25

Ali Returns to the Olympic Games

Opponents who were undefeated

Muhammad Ali faced five opponents in the professional ranks who were, at the time of their contests, undefeated:

    Billy Daniels
    Joe Frazier
    George Foreman
    Leon Spinks
    Larry Holmes

World title holders

During his professional career, Muhammad Ali fought twelve opponents who were or would go on to become a world title holder:

Archie Moore	Undisputed world light-heavyweight champion
Sonny Liston	Undisputed world heavyweight champion
Floyd Patterson	Undisputed world heavyweight champion
Ernie Terrell	WBA world heavyweight champion
Joe Frazier	Undisputed world heavyweight champion
Jimmy Ellis	WBA world heavyweight champion
Bob Foster	Undisputed world light-heavyweight champion
Ken Norton	WBC world heavyweight champion
George Foreman	Undisputed world heavyweight champion
Leon Spinks	Undisputed world heavyweight champion
Larry Holmes	WBC and IBF world heavyweight champion
Trevor Berbick	WBC world heavyweight champion

European heavyweight champions

Muhammad Ali crossed gloves in the ring with seven opponents who had, at one time or another, held the European heavyweight title during their time in the paid ranks:

Jurgen Blin
Joe Bugner
Henry Cooper
Jean-Pierre Coopman
Richard Dunn
Alfredo Evangelista
Karl Mildenberger

Commonwealth heavyweight champions

During his professional career, Muhammad Ali fought five opponents who had at one time or another held the Commonwealth heavyweight title:

Henry Cooper
Brian London
Joe Bugner
Richard Dunn
Trevor Berbick

Four British champions

Muhammad Ali shared the ring with four boxers who had at one time or another held the British title during their careers:

Henry Cooper
Brian London
Joe Bugner
Richard Dunn

Olympic gold medal winners

During his professional career, Ali fought four men in world title bouts who had previously won a gold medal at the Olympic Games:

Floyd Patterson	Middleweight	Helsinki, Finland	1952
Joe Frazier	Heavyweight	Tokyo, Japan	1964
George Foreman	Heavyweight	Mexico City, Mexico	1968
Leon Spinks	Light-heavyweight	Montreal Hall, Canada	1976

Fifteen rounds in world title bouts

During his career, Muhammad Ali went the full distance of fifteen rounds in world heavyweight championship fights more often than any previous title holder at the weight, the total being ten times:

George Chuvalo	29 March 1966
Ernie Terrell	6 February 1967
Joe Frazier	8 March 1971
Joe Bugner	30 June 1975
Jimmy Young	30 April 1976
Ken Norton	28 September 1976
Alfredo Evangelista	16 May 1977
Earnie Shavers	29 September 1977
Leon Spinks	15 February 1978
Leon Spinks	15 September 1978

Muhammad Ali inducted into the International Boxing Hall of Fame

In 1990, Muhammad Ali was honoured when he was inducted into the International Boxing Hall of Fame, in Canastota, New York. Ali more than deserved to take his place with the many other greats in boxing who had participated in the ring over the years.

Ali lights the torch

In 1996, Muhammad Ali appeared at the Olympic Games in Atlanta, USA. On this occasion, he had the honour of lighting the Olympic flame to signal the opening of the Games. The great champion received much applause from the spectators who witnessed the sight. The gold medal winner at light-heavyweight (the weight at which Ali won the gold in the 1960 Games, in Rome, Italy) was Kazakhstan's Vassiliy Jirov.

Don King TV film

Only in America was a 1997 TV film based on promoter Don King. The production also featured many legendary boxers played by various actors. Ving Rhames took on the role of Don King. Muhammad Ali was of course included in the story, played by actor Darius McCrary. The rest of the cast included Bernie Mac as Drew Bundini Brown, Jarrod Bunch as George Foreman, and Israel Cole as Joe Frazier.

Sports Personality of the Century

In 1999, Muhammad Ali was crowned the Sports Personality of the Century by the BBC in their sporting awards ceremony of the millennium. This was no great surprise when considering all of Ali's great accomplishments during his fantastic career. The occasion was attended by other boxers as well as participants from many sports. The choice of Ali was a popular one, welcomed by many.

Chapter 26

The World Bids Farewell to Ali

Ali film

A 2001 film directed by Michael Mann, titled *Ali*, was based on Muhammad Ali's life story and starred Will Smith in the title role. Ron Silver played Angelo Dundee. Jon Voight took on the role of Howard Cosell, Paul Rodriguez portrayed Dr Ferdie Pacheco, Mykelti Williamson played Don King, with Jamie Foxx as Drew Bundini Brown. The cast also included various boxers such as former WBO world heavyweight champion Michael Bentt as Sonny Liston. James Toney, the former IBF world middleweight, super-middleweight and cruiserweight title holder, played Joe Frazier, and Charles Shufford stepped up as George Foreman.

Daughters

On 8 June 2001, at the Turning Stone Resort Casino, Verona, New York, Muhammad Ali's daughter Laila Ali entered the ring to meet Joe Frazier's daughter, Jacqui Frazier-Lyde, in a contest scheduled for eight rounds. Ali came into the battle undefeated in nine bouts whilst Frazier-Lyde entered the ring undefeated in seven bouts. Some critics felt at the time that this was a gimmick contest using their legendary fathers' names as a selling point. This was easy to see why when considering who their fathers were and what had gone before. This, however, was not a cynical case of making a quick buck by cashing in on the Ali and Frazier names. The two ladies revealed that they had skills to be respected and really went for it, giving the fans in attendance an exciting night of boxing. In the early stages of the bout, Ali was unable to contain Frazier-Lyde, who launched an all-out attack.

Ali fought back hard and eventually prevailed when she was awarded the decision on points.

Laila Ali's last professional contest

Laila Ali had her last professional contest on 3 February 2007, stopping challenger Gwendolyn O'Neil in the opening round of ten in defence of her WBC and WIBA world super-middleweight titles. The bout took place at the Emperors Palace, Kempton Park, Gauteng, South Africa. Ali had a successful career, leaving the sport undefeated in twenty-four bouts, winning twenty-one inside the scheduled distance. Ali helped to enhance the cause of women's boxing during her time in the ring.

Eddie Futch

Well-respected trainer and former amateur boxer Eddie Futch died on 10 October 2001. Futch was born on 9 August 1911 in Hillsboro, Mississippi, USA. During his time, he trained many top-notch fighters. Futch knew everything there was to know about boxing. If there was something he did not know, you could rest assured it wasn't worth knowing. He was a master of his trade. Futch is also noted for training four boxers who had defeated Muhammad Ali in the professional ranks during their respected careers: Joe Frazier, Ken Norton, Larry Holmes and Trevor Berbick. There is no doubt that Futch left an outstanding legacy in the sport of boxing.

Presidential Medal of Freedom

In 2005, a further honour was bestowed on the former three-time world heavyweight champion Muhammad Ali when President George W. Bush presented him with the Presidential Medal of Freedom.

Muhammad Ali: The Man Who Changed Boxing

Goodbye to a great

The world said goodbye to the great Muhammad Ali when he died on 3 June 2016, aged 74 years, 4 months and 17 days. His final resting place is at Cave Hill Cemetery, Louisville, Kentucky.

Ferdie Pacheco

Ferdie Pacheco, who was born on 8 December 1927 and died on 16 November 2017, was strongly associated with Muhammad Ali, having served as his ringside physician and cornerman throughout most of the champion's career. Pacheco was a tremendous asset to Ali during his time in the ring, looking after the champ's well-being. Pacheco was known in boxing as the 'fight doctor'.

The grandson of Muhammad Ali

On 14 August 2021, Nico Ali Walsh made his professional debut in the middleweight division when he climbed into the ring at the Hard Rock Hotel and Casino, Tulsa, Oklahoma. His opponent was Jordan Weeks, who had a resume of five bouts, comprising four wins, with one defeat. The contest was scheduled for four rounds but came to a finish in the first stanza, when Walsh stopped his man. Nico Ali Walsh is the grandson of Muhammad Ali. His mother is Rasheda Ali, the daughter of the three-time world heavyweight champion.

The last round

Muhammad Ali
Height   6 feet 3 inches
Reach   78 inches
Nicknames   The Louisville Lip, The Greatest
Boxing stance   Orthodox
Professional record   Sixty-one fights: fifty-six wins, five defeats.

Bibliography

Books

Butler, Frank, *The Good, The Bad and The Ugly: The Story of Boxing*, Stanley Paul, London, 1986
Gutteridge, Reg, *The Big Punchers*, Hutchinson, London, 1983
Myler, Thomas, *Boxing's Greatest Upsets*, Robson Books, London, 1998
Odd, Gilbert, *Boxing: The Great Champions*, Hamlyn, London, 1974

Magazine

Boxing News

Index

A Little Bit of Texas, Saint Louis, Missouri, 129
Agosto, Pedro, 88
Aidala, Artie, 78
Aird, Billy, 115
Aladdin Theatre, Las Vegas, 123
Alderton, John, 101
Ali, Laila, 140–1
Ali, Rahman, 80, 129
Ali, Veronica, 129
Alongi, Tony, 6
Amphitheatre, Reno, Nevada, 42, 72
Anderson, Al, 7
Andrews, Eamonn, 129
Anthony, Tony, 12
Araneta Coliseum, Barangay, Cubao, Quezon City, Metro, Manila, Philippines, 111
Arena, Saint Louis, Missouri, 33, 66
Armory, Jersey City, New Jersey, 43
Arsenal Football Stadium, Highbury, London, 51, 60, 63
Astaire, Fred, 65
Astrodome, Houston, Texas, 64, 67, 81, 82
Auditorium, Miami Beach, Florida, 6–7, 8, 75
Auditorium, Oakland, California, 24
Audubon Country Club, Louisville, Kentucky, 2
August, Bernd, 116

Baer, Buddy, 66
Baer, Max, 34, 35
Baer, Sidney, 6
Bailey, Dave, 43

Banks, Sonny, 15–16, 17, 28, 134, 135
Bay View Park Arena, Toledo, 38
Beatles, The, 31
Beck, Walter, 6
Bellefonte, Harry, 8
Bentt, Michael, 140
Berbick, Trevor, 39, 132–3, 136, 137, 141
Beshore, Freddie, 37
Besmanoff, Willi, 14–15
Billups, Levi, 108
Bingham, Howard, 129
Blin, Jürgen, 82–3, 84, 137
Blue Horizon, Philadelphia, 18
Bodell, Jack, 55, 80
Bonavena, Oscar, 72, 76, 77, 87, 135
Borgnine, Ernest, 122
Boyd, Belinda (Khalilah Ali), 134
Boyd, Jim, 3
Braddock, James J., 34
Briggs, Shannon, 103
Brown, Drew Bundini, 122, 129, 134
Bugner, Joe, 55, 56, 60, 90–1, 94–5, 100–101, 107, 108–109, 116, 118, 137, 138
Bunch, Jarrod, 139
Bung Karno, Stadium, Jakarta, 95
Burman Red, 66
Burns, Tommy, 34, 35, 42, 50, 83
Burton, Tony, 11
Bush, George W., 141
Butler, Alonzo, 133

Caesars Palace, Sports Pavilion, Las Vegas, Nevada, 119, 122, 124, 130, 132
Cameron-Gibbons, Beryl, 101

Index

Cane, Dante, 107
Capital Center, Landover, Maryland, 113, 121
Carnera, Primo, 34, 35, 46
Catholic Youth Center, Scranton, Pennsylvania, 91
Cave Hill Cemetery, Louisville, Kentucky, 142
Centennial Coliseum, Reno, Nevada, 43
Chapman, Claude, 20
Charles, Ezzard, 34, 36, 37, 57, 79, 100
Chicago Stadium, Illinois, 23, 39
Christopher, Jim, 85
Chuvalo, George, 48, 49–50, 51, 67, 74, 81, 85, 138
City Auditorium, Atlanta, Georgia, 75
Civic Arena, Pittsburgh, Pennsylvania, 24
Civic Auditorium, San Francisco, California, 19
Civic Hall, Wolverhampton, West Midlands, 51
Civic Ice Arena, Seattle, Washington, 9
Claremont Hospital, San Diego, 92
Clark, Henry, 89
Clark, LaMar, 9–10, 11
Clay Snr, Cassius, 1, 129
Clay, Odessa Grady, 1, 129
Clay, Rudolph Valentino, 1
Clayton, Zach, 100, 133
Cleroux, Bob, 13, 19
Cobo Arena, Detroit, 89
Cole, Israel, 139
Coliseum, Houston, Texas, 70
Coliseum Arena, Oakland, California, 71
Comiskey Park, Chicago, 46, 57
Comunidad de Madrid, Spain, 122
Coney Island Athletic Club, Brooklyn, New York, 53
Conn, Billy, 66
Convention Center, Atlantic City, New Jersey, 102
Convention Center, Las Vegas, Nevada, 10, 12, 14, 32, 46, 65, 85, 90, 106
Convention Center, Miami Beach, Florida, 7, 8, 17, 72
Convention Center, Philadelphia, Pennsylvania, 66
Convention Hall, Philadelphia, Pennsylvania, 44, 45
Cooney, Gerry, 120
Cooper, Henry, 27–9, 30, 31, 51–2, 53, 56, 58–9, 60, 61, 63, 101, 109, 116, 129, 134, 137
Coopman, Jean-Pierre, 112–13, 137
Corbett, James J., 34, 35, 53, 79
Corletti, Eduardo, 48
Cosell, Howard, 96
Croke Park, Dublin, 87
Crook Jr, Eddie, 3
Cummings, Floyd, 111–12

Daniels, Billy, 17, 20–1, 136
Davies, Dickie, 101
Davila, Roberto, 65
Davis, Jefferson, 51
De Kerpel, Freddy, 113
Dempsey, Jack, 34, 35, 38, 79
Denver Coliseum, Colorado, 65, 123
Derks Field, Salt Lake City, Utah, 10
Dorazio, Gus, 66
Douglas, Billy, 3
Dundee, Angelo, 22, 33, 81, 129
Dundee, Chris, 38
Dunn, Richard, 115, 116–17, 118, 137
Duquesne Gardens, Pittsburgh, Pennsylvania, 36
Durden-Smith, Neil, 101

Eagan, Eddie, 3
Earls Court Arena, Kensington, London, 55, 57, 63, 95
Earls Court Empress Hall, Kensington, 57
Eastern Parkway Arena, Brooklyn, New York, 7
Edson, Jay, 133
El Poliedro in Caracas, Venezuela, 94, 97, 119
Elks Club, Miami, 8
Ellis, Jimmy, 47, 56, 71–2, 73, 79, 81, 85, 88, 129, 136

Muhammad Ali: The Man Who Changed Boxing

Ellis Park Tennis Stadium, Johannesburg, 118
Emperors Palace, Kempton Park, Gauteng, South Africa, 141
Empire Pool, Wembley, London, 27, 55, 56, 60, 61, 63, 86, 89, 115, 117–18
Erskine, Joe, 49, 55
Esch, Eric, 132
Esperti, Tony, 7
Estadio Bristol, Mar del Plata, Buenos Aires, 77
Estadio Luna Park, Buenos Aires, 76, 77, 87
Evangelista, Alfredo, 121–2, 137, 138

Fairgrounds Coliseum, Detroit, Michigan, 3
Fairgrounds Coliseum, Indianapolis, Indiana, 58
Farr, Tommy, 107–108
Faversham, Bill, 5
Felix, Barney, 37
Festhalle, Frankfurt, Germany, 70
Fields, Billy, 11
Finnegan, Chris, 89
Fitzsimmons, Bob, 35, 53, 79
Fleeman, Donnie, 8–9
Folley, Zora, 21, 25, 69, 74, 135
Ford, Duane, 131
Foreman, George, 86, 94, 95–6, 97, 98, 99, 101–102, 103, 104, 111, 114, 119, 136, 138
Forum, Montreal, Canada, 13
Forum, The Inglewood, California, 93
Foster, Bob, 25, 86, 88–9, 136
Foster, Mac, 70, 84
Foxx, Jamie, 140
Frank, Scott, 105
Frazier, Joe, 26, 44, 71, 72–3, 77–8, 79, 81, 82, 88, 89, 95–6, 97, 98, 110, 111–12, 113, 121, 129, 134, 135, 136, 138, 140, 141
Frazier-Lyde, Jacqui, 140
Freedom Hall, Louisville, Kentucky, 5, 9, 12, 13, 14
Funkturmhalle, Westend, Berlin, 14

Furch, Dave, 24
Futch, Eddie, 141

Garcia, José Luis, 91
Gardner, John L., 115
Garrett, Chuck, 16
General Hospital, Louisville, Kentucky, 1
Ghent, Province of Oost-Vlaanderen, Belgium, 113
Gibbs, Harry, 59, 63
Giorgetti, José, 77
Gleason, Jackie, 23
Goldstein, Ruby, 17
Goss, Woody, 44
Gray, Clyde, 133
Graystone Ballroom, Detroit, Michigan, 16
Green, Richard, 131
Griffith Stadium, Washington, District of Columbia, 66
Grosvenor House Sporting Club, Mayfair, London, 115
Gutteridge, Reg, 101

Hallenstadion, Zurich, 83, 84
Hamburg, Germany, 83
Hampton, John, 2
Hard Rock Hotel & Casino, Tulsa, Oklahoma, 142
Harringay Arena, London, 27, 57
Harris, Julie, 23
Harris, Stamford, 75
Hart, Colin, 101
Hart, Marvin, 34, 35, 42, 50, 72
Harvey, Len, 101
Herring, Todd, 46, 64
Hillsboro, Mississippi, 141
Hilton Hotel, Las Vegas, 39, 125
Hinke, Terry, 104
Ho-Chunk Casino, Baraboo, Wisconsin, 125
Holmes, Larry, 91, 119, 122, 124–5, 128, 130–1, 132, 136, 141
Holyfield, Evander, 102
Honolulu International Center, Hawaii, 106

Index

Houpe, Fred, 129
Hubbard, Alan, 101
Hunsaker, Tunney, 5, 6

Ice Rink, Nottingham, 55
Ice World, Totowa, New Jersey, 105
Inoki, Antonio, 118
International Amphitheatre, Chicago, Illinois, 44, 67, 111
International Boxing Hall of Fame, 138
International Hotel and Casino, Las Vegas, 82

Jacobson, Gus, 37
Jeffries, James J., 34, 35, 42, 53, 79
Jerome, George, 50
Jirov, Vassiliy, 139
Joe Louis Arena, Detroit, Michigan, 128
Johansson, Ingemar, 8, 34, 35, 46, 79, 98
Johnson, Alonzo, 12–13
Johnson, Amos, 43, 58
Johnson, George, 83
Johnson, Harold, 25
Johnson, Jack, 34, 35, 36, 50, 83–4
Jones, Doug, 25–6, 67, 135
Jones, Ken, 101
Jones, Tom, 129
Joyner, Floyd, 69
Jupiters Hotel and Casino, Broadbeach, Queensland, Australia, 108

Kataoka, Noboru, 84
Kessler, Harry, 68
Kiel Auditorium, Saint Louis, Missouri, 36
King, Ben E., 40
King, Bill, 5
King, Don, 111, 131
King, Howard, 14
Kings Hall, Belle Vue, Manchester, 55, 57
Kiselyov, Aleksei, 4
Knight, Billy, 101
Knoetze, Kallie, 118
Kristofferson, Kris, 130
Kyobashi Hall, Tokyo, 84

LA Sports Arena, 22
Lavorante, Alejandro, 11, 21–2
Lawlor Events Center, Reno, Nevada, 128
Lee, Norvel, 3
Levene, Harry, 52–3
Lewis, Al (Blue), 87
Lewis, Laurie, 58
Liston, Sonny, 27, 31, 32–3, 34, 35, 36, 38, 39, 40–1, 42, 43, 44, 45, 46, 51, 67, 72, 79, 82, 136
Little, Tommy, 30
Lockton, Dennis, 57
Logan, George, 19
London, Brian, 55, 57–8, 59, 60, 63, 90, 116, 137
London Palladium, 29
Louis, Joe, 1, 34, 35, 57, 79, 107–108
Lovell, Alberto, 100
Lovett, Bunny, 37
Lubbers, Rudi, 94–5
Lyle, Ron, 106, 123

McAlinden, Danny, 80, 117
McCarter, Jimmy, 13
McCary, Darius, 139
McClure, Wilbert, 3
McDonald, Bill, 38
McGhee, Frank, 101
McMurray, Bill, 43
McNair, Jimmy, 25
McNeeley, Tom, 42, 49
Mac, Bernie, 139
Machen, Eddie, 44, 67
Madigan, Anthony, 3
Madison Square Garden, New York, 15, 17, 25–6, 28, 66, 69–70, 71, 72, 74, 76, 77, 82, 84, 88, 95, 102, 120, 123, 134
Manchester, Dr Gary, 92
Mancini, Terry, 101
Mann, Michael, 140
Maple Leaf Gardens, Toronto, Canada, 42, 48, 49, 67, 81, 85
Marciano, Rocky, 23, 34, 35, 39, 73–4
Marigold Gardens, Chicago, Illinois, 16
Marley, John, 122

Muhammad Ali: The Man Who Changed Boxing

Marshall, Marty, 36
Martin Joe E., 1, 6, 129
Martin, Leotis, 72, 81–2
Matchuny, Paul, 6
Mathis, Buster, 71, 82
Memorial Auditorium, Buffalo, New York, 37
Memorial Auditorium, Sacramento, California, 11
Mercante Snr, Arthur, 78
Merdeka Stadium, Kula Lumpur, 107
Merritt, Jeff, 69
MGM Grand, Las Vegas, 103
MGM Grand Garden Arena, Las Vegas, 102
Middleton, Larry, 86
Mildenberger, Karl, 61–2, 63, 70, 72, 83, 117, 137
Minker, Chuck, 131
Mission Street Arena, Colma, California, 42
Mississippi Coast Coliseum, Biloxi, California, 115
Miteff, Alex, 12, 13–14
Molineux Grounds, Wolverhampton, 55
Moore, Archie, 21–2, 23, 38, 39, 136
Moorer, Michael, 102–103
Morrison, Tommy, 102
Mosley, Roger E., 122
Motor City, Arena, Detroit, Michigan, 36
Municipal Stadium, Philadelphia, Pennsylvania, 100
Musto, Tony, 66

Nakagoshi, Yutaka, 84
Nassau Coliseum, Uniondale, New York, 111
National Stadium, Kingston, Jamaica, 96
Naud Junction Pavilion, Los Angeles, California, 42
Nippon Budokan, Tokyo, 84, 97, 118
Norton, Ken, 89–90, 91, 92, 93, 94, 95, 97, 118–19, 120, 121, 127, 130, 136, 138, 141
Nova, Lou, 66

O'Brien, Philadelphia Jack, 42
O'Halloran, Jack, 80
O'Jones, Barbara, 130
O'Keefe, Ronnie, 2, 129
O'Neal, Ron, 130
O'Neil, Gwendolyn, 141
Olympia, Kensington, London, 48
Olympia Stadium, Detroit, Michigan, 66
Olympiahalle, Munich, Germany, 116
Olympic Auditorium, Los Angeles, 11, 13, 21, 24, 91
Olympic Club, New Orleans, Louisiana, 35
Olympic gold medal, 2
Oriental Park, Havana, Cuba, 84

Pacheco, Dr Ferdie, 142
Pacific Athletic Club, Los Angeles, 50
Paez, Miguel Angel, 77
Painter, Harry, 27
Palacio de los Deportes, Madrid, Spain, 116
Palazzetto dello Sport, Bologna, Italy, 107
Palisades Rink, McKeesport, Pennsylvania, 12
Parkinson's disease, 133–4
Paschall, Orie, 18
Pastrano, Willie, 22
Patterson, Floyd, 8, 23, 34, 35, 36, 38, 39, 42, 45–7, 49, 51, 58, 63, 65, 71, 72, 79, 88, 98, 135, 136, 138
Phantom Punch, 41
Philadelphia Arena, Pennsylvania, 25–6, 64
Pietrzykowski, Zbigniew, 2, 3, 4, 129
Pires, Luis Faustino, 76
Polo Grounds, New York, 66, 98
Polo Grounds, Palm Springs, California, 11, 46
Porsche, Veronica, 134
Potter, Carl, 115
Powell, Charlie, 24
Prescott, Johnny, 55
Presley, Elvis, 90

Index

Qawi, Dwight Muhammad, 128
Quarry, Jerry, 71–2, 74, 75, 76, 82, 84, 85–6
Quarry, Mike, 86
Queen Elizabeth Sports Centre, Nassau, Bahamas, 132
Quinn, Anthony, 23

Race Track Arena, Carson City, Nevada, 53
Rademacher, Pete, 9, 10
Råsunda Fotbollsstadion, Stockholm, 47, 88
Recht, Bill, 78
Regency Hotel, Denver, Colorado, 106
Reno, Charlie, 91
Rhames, Ving, 139
Richardson, Dick, 27, 55
Richfield Coliseum, Ohio, 104
Rigetti, Alfio, 125
Riggins, John, 24
Roberto Clemente Coliseum, San Juan, Puerto Rico, 112, 113–14
Robinson, Jimmy, 8
Rodriguez, Paul, 140
Roi, Sonji, 134
Roman, José, 97, 113
Rooney, Mickey, 23
Root, Jack, 42, 72
Ros Giuseppe, 84
Royal Albert Hall, Kensington, London, 94, 100, 116
Rudolph, Wilma, 129
Rush, Elmer, 43

Sabedong, Duke, 11–12
Sahara Tahoe Hotel, Stateline, Nevada, 89
Salt Palace, Salt Lake City, Utah, 104
Sam Houston Coliseum, Houston, Texas, 26, 64, 67
San Diego, California, 80, 91
Saraudi, Giulio, 3
Savold, Lee, 34, 35, 56–7
Schmeling, Max, 34, 35, 62, 79
Schreiber, Heinz, 14

Schulz, Axel, 103
Scope Arena, Norfolk, Virginia, 132
Selland Arena, Fresno, California, 70
Shain, Eva, 124
Sharkey, Jack, 34, 62
Shatkov, Gennadiy, 2–3
Shavers, Earnie, 123–4, 125, 135, 138
Shufford, Charles, 140
Siler, Herb, 6–7
Silver, Ron, 140
Simon, Abe, 66
Sinatra, Frank, 79
Singer Bowl, Flushing Meadows, Queens, New York, 88
Slaughter, Dave, 106
Smith, Don, 33
Smith, George, 53
Smith, Howard, 123
Smith, Will, 140
Solomons, Jack, 30, 58–9
Spencer, Thad, 57, 72
Spinks, Leon, 119, 125–6, 127, 128, 129, 130, 136, 138
Sports Arena, Los Angeles, 18, 21
Sports Arena, San Diego, 91
Squires, Bill, 42
St Andrews (Birmingham City FC), Birmingham, 55
St Lawrence Market, Toronto, 50
St Nicholas Arena, New York, 12, 17, 20
Stade du 20 Mai, Kinshasa, Democratic Republic of the Congo, 97
Stadium, The, Liverpool, 58
Stallone, Sylvester, 105
Steele, Richard, 131
Stevens, Les, 115
Stewart, Ed, 101
Stoner, Fred, 129
Stru, Tommy, 6
Sullivan, John L., 34, 35
Superdome, New Orleans, Louisiana, 127
Sydney Stadium, New South Wales, Australia, 50, 83

Taj Majal hotel and casino, Atlantic City, New Jersey, 103
Terrell, Ernie, 26, 44, 48, 64, 67–8, 69, 70, 72, 136, 138
Thomas, Clay, 16
Thomas & Mack Center, Las Vegas, Nevada, 102
Toney, James, 140
Tucker, Tony, 103
Tunney, Gene, 34, 62
Turning Stone Resort Casino, Verona, New York, 140
Tyson, Mike, 39

Urtain, José Manuel, 116

Vasile, Tiţă, 39
Villa Park, Birmingham, 80
Voight, Jon, 140

Wagner, Raymond George, 31
Wakelin, Johnny, 100
Walcott, Jersey Joe, 34, 35, 36, 42, 57, 79, 100
Waldhelm, Don, 102
Waldstadion/Radrennbahn, Frankfurt, Germany, 61, 83
Walker, Billy, 55
Walsh, Nico Ali, 142

Waltham, Teddy, 62
Warner, Don, 17–18
WAVE-TV Studio, Louisville, Kentucky, 2
Weeks, Jordan, 142
Welch, Julie, 101
Wembley Stadium, London, 27, 31
Wepner, Chuck, 43, 104–105, 134
White City Stadium, London, 57
Wilburn, Chuck, 10
Willard, Jess, 34, 35, 38, 84
Williams, Cleveland, 64–5, 66, 68
Williams, Yolanda 'Lonnie', 134
Williamson, Mykelti, 140
Winnipeg Arena, Manitoba Pacific Coliseum, 85
Woodcock, Bruce, 56–7
World Sporting Club, Mayfair, 115
Wright, Arthur, 122

X, Cassius, 40

Yankee Stadium, Bronx, New York, 23, 46, 62, 108, 119
Yates, Brian, 125
Young, Jimmy, 106, 113–14, 115, 119, 138

Zech, Gerhard, 43